AUDIO-VISION

· · ·

AUDIO-VISION

• • •

SOUND ON SCREEN

Michel Chion

• • •

edited and

translated by

Claudia Gorbman

with a foreword by

Walter Murch

COLUMBIA UNIVERSITY PRESS • NEW YORK

Columbia University Press wishes to express its appreciation of assistance given by the government of France through Le Ministère de la Culture in the preparation of the translation.

•   •   •

Columbia University Press

New York   Chichester, West Sussex

L'Audio-Vision © 1990 Editions Nathan, Paris

Library of Congress Cataloging-in-Publication Data

Chion, Michel

[Audio-vision. French]

Audio-vision: sound on screen/Michel Chion; edited and translated by Claudia Gorbman; with a foreword by Walter Murch.

p.   cm

Includes bibliographical references and index.

ISBN 0-231-07898-6

ISBN 0-231-07899-4 (pbk.)

1. Sound motion pictures.   2. Motion pictures—Sound effects. 3. Motion pictures—Aesthetics.   I. Gorbman, Claudia.   II. Murch, Walter, 1943–   . III. Title.

PN1995.7.C4714   1994

791.43'024—dc20   93-23982

CIP

CONTENTS

FOREWORD

WALTER MURCH

. . .

We gestate in Sound, and are born into Sight
Cinema gestated in Sight, and was born into Sound.

     We begin to hear before we are born, four and a half months after conception. From then on, we develop in a continuous and luxurious bath of sounds: the song of our mother's voice, the swash of her breathing, the trumpeting of her intestines, the timpani of her heart. Throughout the second four-and-a-half months, Sound rules as solitary Queen of our senses: the close and liquid world of uterine darkness makes Sight and Smell impossible, Taste monochromatic, and Touch a dim and generalized hint of what is to come.

Birth brings with it the sudden and simultaneous ignition of the other four senses, and an intense competition for the throne that Sound had claimed as hers. The most notable pretender is the darting and insistent Sight, who dubs himself King as if the throne had been standing vacant, waiting for him.

Ever discreet, Sound pulls a veil of oblivion across her reign and withdraws into the shadows, keeping a watchful eye on the braggart Sight. If she gives up her throne, it is doubtful that she gives up her crown.

In a mechanistic reversal of this biological sequence, Cinema spent its youth (1892—-1927) wandering in a mirrored hall of voiceless images, a thirty-five year bachelorhood over which Sight ruled as self-satisfied, solipsistic King—never suspecting that destiny was preparing an arranged marriage with the Queen he thought he had deposed at birth.

This cinematic inversion of the natural order may be one of the reasons that the analysis of sound in films has always been peculiarly elusive and problematical, if it was attempted at all. In fact, despite her dramatic entrance in 1927, Queen Sound has glided around the hall mostly ignored even as she has served us up her delights, while we continue to applaud King sight on his throne. If we do notice her consciously, it is often only because of some problem or defect.

Such self-effacement seems at first paradoxical, given the power of sound and the undeniable technical progress it has made in the last sixty-five years. A further examination of the source of this power, however, reveals it to come in large part from the very handmaidenly quality of self-effacement itself: by means of some mysterious perceptual alchemy, whatever virtues sound brings to the film are largely perceived and appreciated by the audience in *visual* terms—the better the sound, the better the image. The

French composer, filmmaker, and theoretician Michel Chion has dedicated a large part of *Audio-Vision* to drawing out the various aspects of this phenomenon—which he terms *added value*—and this alchemy also lies at the heart of his three earlier, as-yet-untranslated works on film sound: *Le Son au cinéma, La Voix au cinéma*, and *La Toile trouée*. It gives me great pleasure to be able to introduce this author to the American public, and I hope it will not be long before his other works are also translated and published.

It is symptomatic of the elusive and shadowy nature of film sound that Chion's four books stand relatively alone in the landscape of film criticism, representing as they do a significant portion of everything that has ever been published about film sound from a theoretical point of view. For it is also part of Sound's effacement that she respectfully declines to be interviewed, and previous writers on film have with uncharacteristic circumspection largely respected her wishes.

It is also characteristic that this silence has been broken by a European rather than an American—even though sound for films was an American invention, and nearly all of the subsequent developments (including the most recent Dolby SR-D digital soundtrack) have been American or Anglo-American. As fish are the last to become aware of the water in which they swim, Americans take their sound for granted. But such was—and is—not the case in Europe, where the invasion of sound from across the Atlantic in 1927 was decidedly a mixed blessing and something of a curse: not without reason is chapter 7 of *Audio-Vision* (on the arrival of sound) ironically subheaded "Sixty Years of Regrets."

There are several reasons for Europe's ambivalent reaction to film sound, but the heart of the problem was foreshadowed by Faust in 1832, when Goethe had him proclaim:

> It is written that in the Beginning was the Word!
> Hmm . . . *already* I am having problems.

The early sound films were preeminently *talking* films, and the Word—with all of the power that language has to divide nation from nation as well as conquer individual hearts—has long been both the Achilles' heel of Europe as well as its crowning glory. In 1927 there were over twenty different languages spoken in Europe by two hundred million people in twenty-five different, highly developed countries. Not to mention different dialects and accents within each language and a number of countries such as Switzerland and Belgium that are multilingual.

Silent films, however, which blossomed during and after the First World War, were Edenically oblivious of the divisive powers of the Word, and were thus able—when they so desired—to speak to Europe as a whole. It is true that most of these films had intertitle cards, but these were easily and routinely switched according to the language of the country in which the film was being shown.

Even so, title cards were generally discounted as a necessary evil and there were some films, like those of writer Carl Mayer (*The Last Laugh*), that managed to tell their story without any cards at all and were highly esteemed for this ability, which was seen as the wave of the future.

It is also worth recalling that at that time the largest studio in Europe was Nordisk Films in Denmark, a country whose population of two million souls spoke a language understood nowhere else. And Asta Nielsen, the Danish star who made many films for Ufa Studios in Germany, was beloved equally by French and German soldiers during the 1914–18 war—her picture decorated the trenches on both sides. It is doubtful that the French poet Apollinaire, if he had heard her speaking in German, would have written his ode to her—

She is all!
She is the vision of the drinker and the dream of the lonely man!

—but since she hovered in shimmering and enigmatic silence, the dreaming soldiers could imagine her speaking any language they wished and make of her their sister or their lover according to their needs.

So the hopeful spirit of the League of Nations, which flourished for a while after the War That Was Supposed to End All Wars, seemed to be especially served by many of the films of the period, which—in their creative struggle to overcome the disability of silence—rose above the particular and spoke to those aspects of the human condition that know no national boundaries: Chaplin was adopted as a native son by each of the countries in which his films were shown. Some optimists even dared to think of film as a providential tool delivered in the nick of time to help unite humanity in peace: a new, less material tower erected by a modern Babel. The main studios of Ufa in Germany were in fact located in a suburb of Berlin named Neubabelsberg (new Babel city).

Thus it was with a sense of queasy forboding that many film lovers in Europe heard the approaching drumbeat of Sound. Chaplin held out, resisting a full soundtrack for his films until—significantly—*The Great Dictator* (1938). As it acquired a voice, the Tool for Peace began more to resemble the Gravedigger's Spade that had helped to dig the trenches of nationalist strife.

There were of course many more significant reasons for the rise of the Great Dictators in the twenties and thirties, and it is true that the silent film had sometimes been used to rally people around the flag, but it is nonetheless chilling to recall that Hitler's ascension to power marched in lockstep with the successful development of the talking film. And, of course, precisely because it did emphasize language, the sound film dovetailed with the divisive nationalist agendas of Hitler, Stalin, Mussolini, Franco, and others. Hitler's first public act after his victory in 1933 was to attend a screening of *Dawn*, a sound film about the German side of the 1914—18 conflict, in which one of the soldiers says, "Perhaps we Germans do not know how to live; but to die, that we know how to do incredibly well."

Alongside these political implications, the coming of sound allowed the American studios to increase their economic presence in Europe and accelerated the flight of the most talented and promising continental filmmakers (Lubitsch, Lang, Freund, Wilder, Zinnemann, etc.) to distant Hollywood. Neubabelsberg suffered the same fate as its Biblical namesake. To further sour the marriage, the first efforts at sound itself were technically poor, unimaginative, and expensive—the result of American patents that had to be purchased. Early sound recording apparatus also straitjacketed the camera and consequently impoverished the visual richness and fluidity that had been attained in the mature films of the silent era. Nordisk Films collapsed. The studios that were left standing, facing rising production costs and no longer able to count on a market outside the borders of their own country, had to accept some form of government assistance to survive, with all that such assistance implies. Studios in the United States, on the other hand, were insulated by an eager domestic audience three times the size of the largest single European market, all conveniently speaking the same language. As the United States was spared the bloodshed on its soil in both world wars, it was spared the conflict of the sound wars and, in fact, managed to profit by them.

Sixty-five years later, the reverberations of this political, cultural, and economic trauma still echo throughout Europe in an unsettled critical attitude toward film sound—and a multitude of aesthetic approaches—that have no equivalent in the United States: compare Chion's description of the French passion for "location" sound at all costs (Eric Rohmer) with the Italian reluctance to use it under any circumstances (Fellini). This is not to say that Chion, as a European, shares the previously mentioned regrets—just the opposite: he is an ardent admirer and proponent of soundtracks from both sides of the Atlantic—but as a European he is naturally more sensitive to the economic, cultural, political, and aesthetic ramifications of the marriage of Sight and Sound. And since the initial audience for his books and articles has also— until now—been European, part of his task has been to convince his wary continental readers of the artistic merits of film sound (the French word for sound effect, for instance, is *bruit*—which translates as "noise," with all of the same pejorative overtones that the word has in English) and to persuade them to forgive Sound the guilt by association of having been present at the bursting of the silent film's illusory bubble of peace. American readers of this book should therefore be aware that they are—in part— eavesdropping on the latest stage of a family discussion that has been simmering in Europe, with various degrees of acrimony, since the marriage of Sight and Sound was consummated in 1927.

Yet a European perspective does not, by itself, yield a book like *Audio-Vision*: Chion's efforts to explore and synthesize a comprehensive theory of film sound—rather than polemicize it—are largely unprecedented even in Europe. There is another aspect to all this, which the following story might illuminate.

In the early 1950s, when I was around ten years old, and inexpensive magnetic tape recorders were first becoming available, I heard a rumor that the father of a neighborhood friend had actually acquired one. Over the next few months, I made a pest of myself at that household, showing up with a variety of excuses just to be allowed to play with that miraculous machine: hanging the microphone out the window and capturing the back-alley reverberations of Manhattan, Scotchtaping it to the shaft of a swing-arm lamp and rapping the bell-shaped shade with pencils, inserting it into one end of a vacuum cleaner tube and shouting into the other, and so forth.

Later on, I managed to convince my parents of all the money our family would save on records if we bought our own tape recorder and used it to "pirate" music off the radio. I now doubt that they believed this made any economic sense, but they could hear the passion in my voice, and a Revere recorder became that year's family Christmas present.

I swiftly appropriated the machine into my room and started banging on lamps again and resplicing my recordings in different, more exotic combinations. I was in heaven, but since no one else I knew shared this vision of paradise, a secret doubt about myself began to worm its way into my preadolescent thoughts.

One evening, though, I returned home from school, turned on the radio in the middle of a program, and couldn't believe my ears: sounds were being broadcast the likes of which I had only heard in the secrecy of my own little laboratory. As quickly as possible, I connected the recorder to the radio and sat there listening, rapt, as the reels turned and the sounds became increasingly strange and wonderful.

It turned out to be the *Premier Panorama de Musique Concrète*, a record by the French composers Pierre Schaeffer and Pierre Henry, and the incomplete tape of it became a sort of Bible of Sound for me. Or rather a Rosetta stone, because the vibrations chiseled into its iron oxide were the mysteriously significant and powerful hieroglyphs of a language that I did not yet understand but whose voice nonetheless spoke to me compellingly. And above all told me that I was not alone in my endeavors.

Those preadolescent years that I spent pickling myself in my jar of sound, listening and recording and splicing without reference to any image, allowed me—when I eventually came to film—to see through Sound's handmaidenly self-effacement and catch more than a glimpse of her crown.

I mention this fragment of autobiography because apparently Michel Chion came to his interest in film sound through a similar sequence of events. Such a "biological" approach—sound first, image later—stands in contrast not only to the way most people approach film—image first, sound later—but, as we have seen, to the history of cinema itself. As it turns out, Chion is a brother not only in this but also in having Schaeffer and Henry as mentors (although he has the privilege, which I lack, of a long-standing personal contact with those composers), and I was happy to see Schaeffer's name and some of his theories woven into the fabric of *Audio-Vision*. At any rate, I suspect that a primary emphasis on sound for its own sake—combined in Chion's case with a European perspective—must have provided the right mixture of elements to inspire him to knock on reclusive Sound's door, and to see his suitor's determination rewarded with armfuls of intimate details.

What had conquered me in 1953, what had conquered Schaeffer and Henry some years earlier, and what was to conquer Chion in turn was not just the considerable power of magnetic tape to capture ordinary sounds and reorganize them—optical film and discs had already had something of this ability for decades—but the fact that the tape recorder combined these qualities with full audio fidelity, low surface noise, unrivaled accessibility, and operational simplicity. The earlier forms of sound recording had been expensive, available to only a few people outside the laboratory or studio situations, noisy and deficient in their frequency range, and cumbersome and awkward to operate. The tape recorder, on the other hand, encouraged play and experimentation, and that was—and remains—its preeminent virtue.

For as far back in human history as you would care to go, sounds had seemed to be the inevitable and "accidental" (and therefore mostly ignored) accompaniment of the visual—stuck like a shadow to the object that caused them. And, like a shadow, they appeared to be completely explained by reference to the objects that gave them birth: a metallic clang was always "cast" by the hammer, just as the smell of baking always came from a loaf of fresh bread.

Recording magically lifted the shadow away from the object and stood it on its own, giving it a miraculous and sometimes frightening substantiality. King Ndombe of the Congo consented to have his voice recorded in 1904, but immediately regretted it when the cylinder was played back and the "shadow" danced, and he heard his people cry in dismay, "The King sits still, his lips are sealed, while the white man forces his soul to sing!"

The tape recorder extended this magic by an order of magnitude, and made it supremely democratic in the bargain, such that a ten-year-old boy like myself could think of it as a wonderful toy. Furthermore, it was now not only possible but easy to change the original sequence of the recorded sounds, speed them up, slow them down, play them backward. Once the shadow of sound had learned to dance, we found ourselves able to not only listen to the sounds themselves, liberated from their original causal connection, and to layer them in new, formerly impossible recombinations (*Musique Concrète*) but also—in cinema—to reassociate those sounds with images of objects or situations that were different, sometimes astonishingly different, than the objects or situations that gave birth to the sounds in the first place.

And here is the problem: the shadow that had heretofore either been ignored or consigned to follow along submissively behind the image was suddenly running free, or attaching itself mischievously to the unlikeliest things. And our culture, which is not an "auditive" one, had never developed the concepts or language to adequately describe or cope with such an unlikely challenge from such a mercurial force—as Chion points out: "There is always something about sound that bypasses and surprises us, no matter what we do." In retrospect, it is no wonder that few have dared to confront the dancing shadow and the singing soul: it is this deficiency that Michel Chion's *Audio-Vision* bravely sets out to rectify.

The essential first step that Chion takes is to assume that there is no "natural and preexisting harmony between image and sound"—that the shadow is in fact dancing free. In his usual succinct manner, Robert Bresson captured the same idea: "Images and sounds, like strangers who make acquaintance on a journey and afterwards cannot separate."

The challenge that an idea like this presents to the filmmaker is how to create the right situations and make the right choices so that bonds of seeming inevitability are forged between the film's images and sounds, while admitting that there was nothing inevitable about them to begin with. The "journey" is the film, and the particular "acquaintance" lasts within the context of that film: it did not preexist and is perfectly free to be reformed differently on subsequent trips.

The challenge to a theoretician like Chion, on the other hand, is how to define—as broadly but as precisely as possible—the circumstances under which the "acquaintance" can be made, has been made in the past, and might best be made in the future. This challenge Chion takes up in the first six chapters of *Audio-Vision* in the form of an "Audiovisual Contract"—a synthesis and further extension of the theories developed over the last ten years in his previous three books. I should mention that as a result this section has a structural and conceptual density that may require closer attention than the second part (chapters 7–10: "Beyond Sounds and Images"), which is more freely discursive.

In the course of drawing up his contract, Chion quickly runs into the limits of ordinary language (English as well as French) to describe certain aspects of sound. This is to be expected, given the fact that we are trying to trap a shadow behind the bars of a contract, but in the process Chion forges a number of original words that give him at least a fighting chance: *synchresis, spatial magnetization, acousmatic sound, reduced listening, rendered sound, sound "en creux," the phantom of the Acousmêtre*, and so on—even *audio-vision* itself, which acquires a new meaning beyond the obvious.

Some of these terms represent concepts that will be familiar to those of us who work in film sound, but which we have either never had to articulate or for which we have developed our own individual shorthand—or for which we resort to grunts and gestures. It was a pleasure to see these old friends dressed up in new clothes, so to speak, and to have the opportunity to reevaluate them free of old or unstated assumptions. By the same token, other of Chion's ideas are, for me, completely new and original ways of thinking about the subject—in that regard I was particularly impressed by the concept of the "Acousmêtre." But the real achievement of *Audio-Vision* is—beyond simply naming and describing these isolated ideas and concepts—that it manages to synthesize them into a coherent whole whose overall pattern makes it accessible to interested nonprofessionals as well as those who have experience in the craft.

We take it for granted that this dancing shadow of sound, once free of the object that created it, can then reattach itself to a wide range of other objects and images. The sound of an ax chopping wood, for instance, played exactly in sync with a bat hitting a baseball, will "read" as a particularly forceful hit rather than a mistake by the filmmakers. Chion's term for this phenomenon is *synchresis*, an acronym formed by the telescoping together of the two words *synchronism* and *synthesis*: "The spontaneous and irresistible mental fusion, completely free of any logic, that happens between a sound and a visual when these occur at exactly the same time."

It might have been otherwise—the human mind could have demanded absolute obedience to "the truth"—but for a range of practical and aesthetic reasons we are lucky that it didn't: the possibility of reassociation of image and sound is the fundamental stone upon which the rest of the edifice of film sound is built, and without which it would collapse.

This reassociation is done for many reasons: sometimes in the interests of making a sound appear more "real" than reality (what Chion calls *rendered sound)*—walking on cornstarch, for instance, records as a better footstep in snow than snow itself; sometimes it is done simply for convenience (cornstarch, again) or necessity— the window that Gary Cooper broke in *High Noon* was not made of real glass, the boulder that chased Indiana Jones was not made of real stone, or morality—the sound of a watermelon being crushed instead of a human head. In each case, our species' multimillion-year habit of thinking of sound as a submissive shadow now works in a filmmaker's favor, and the audience is disposed to accept, within certain limits, these new juxtapositions as the truth.

But beyond all practical considerations, this reassociation is done—should be done, I believe—to *stretch* the relationship of sound to image wherever possible: to create a purposeful and fruitful tension between what is on the screen and what is kindled in the mind of the audience—what Chion calls sound *en creux* (sound "in the gap"). The danger of present-day cinema is that it can crush its subjects by its very ability to represent them; it doesn't possess the built-in escape valves of ambiguity that painting, music, literature, radio drama, and black-and-white silent film automatically have simply by virtue of their sensory incompleteness—an incompleteness that engages the imagination of the viewer as compensation for what is only evoked by the artist. By comparison, film seems to be "all there" (it isn't, but it seems to be), and thus the responsibility of filmmakers is to find ways within that completeness to refrain from achieving it. To that end, the metaphoric use of sound is one of the most fruitful, flexible, and inexpensive means: by choosing carefully what to eliminate, and then reassociating different sounds that seem at first hearing to be somewhat at odds with the accompanying image, the film-maker can open up a perceptual vacuum into which the mind of the audience must inevitably rush.

It is this movement "into the vacuum" (or "into the gap," to use Chion's phrase) that is in all probability the source of the added value mentioned earlier. Every successful metaphor—what Aristotle called "naming a thing with that which is not its name"—is seen initially and briefly as a mistake, but then suddenly as a deeper truth about the thing named and our relationship to it. And the greater the metaphoric distance, or gap, between image and accompanying sound, the greater the value added—within certain limits. The slippery thing in all this is that there seems to be a peculiar "stealthy" quality to this added value: it chooses not to acknowledge its origins in the mind.

The tension produced by the metaphoric distance between sound and image serves somewhat the same purpose, creatively, as the perceptual tension produced by the physical distance between our two eyes—a three-inch gap that yields two similar but *slightly different* images: one produced by the left eye and the other by the right. The brain is not content with this close duality and searches for something that would resolve and unify those differences. And it finds it in the concept of depth. By adding its own purely mental version of three-dimensionality to the two flat images, the brain causes them to click together into one image with depth added. In other words, the brain resolves the differences between the two images by imagining a dimensionality that is not actually present in either image but added as the result of a mind trying to resolve the differences between them. As before, the greater the differences, the greater the depth. (Again, within certain limits: cross your eyes—exaggerating the differences—and you will deliver images to the brain that are beyond its power to resolve, and so it passes on to you, by default, a confusing double image. Close one eye—eliminate the differences—and the brain will give you a flat image with no confusion, but also with no value added.)

There really is of course some kind of depth out there in the world: the dimensionality we perceive is not a hallucination. But the *way* we perceive it—its particular flavor—is uniquely our own, unique not only to us as a species but to each of us individually. And in that sense it *is* a kind of hallucination, because the brain does not alert us to the process: it does not announce, "And now I am going to add a helpful dimensionality to synthesize these two flat images. Don't be alarmed." Instead, the dimensionality is fused into the image and made to seem as if it is coming from out there rather than "in here."

In much the same way, the mental effort of fusing image and sound in a film produces a "dimensionality" that the mind projects back onto the image as if it had come from the image in the first place. The result is that we see something on the *screen* that exists only in our minds, and is in its finer details unique to each member of the audience. It reminds me of John Huston's observation that "the real projectors are the eyes and ears of the audience." Despite all appearances, we do not *see* and *hear* a film, we *hear/see* it—hence the title of Chion's book: *Audio-Vision*. The difference is the time it takes: the fusion of left and right eye into three dimensions takes place instantly because the distance between our eyes does not change. On the other hand the metaphoric distance between the images of a film and the accompanying sounds is—and should be—continuously changing and flexible, and it takes a good number of milliseconds (or sometimes even seconds) for the brain to make the right connections. The image of a door closing accompanied simply by the sound of a door closing is fused almost instantly and produces a relatively flat "audio-vision"; the image of a half-naked man alone in a Saigon hotel room accompanied by the sound of jungle birds (to use an example from *Apocalypse Now*) takes longer to fuse but is a more "dimensional" audio-vision when it succeeds.

I might add that, in my own experience, the most successful sounds seem not only to alter what the audience sees but to go further and trigger a kind of *conceptual resonance* between image and sound: the sound makes us see the image differently, and then this new image makes us hear the sound differently, which in turn makes us see something else in the image, which makes us hear different things in the sound, and so on. This happens rarely enough (I am thinking of certain electronic sounds at the beginning of *The Conversation*) to be specially prized when it does occur—often by lucky accident, dependent as it is on choosing exactly the right sound at exactly the right metaphoric distance from the image. It has something to do with the time it takes for the audience to "get" the metaphors: not instantaneously, but not much delayed either—like a good joke.

The question remains, in all of this, why we generally perceive the product of the fusion of image and sound—the audio-vision—in terms of the image. In other words, why does King Sight still sit on his throne?

One of Chion's most original observations—the phantom Acousmêtre—depends for its effect on delaying the fusion of sound and image to the extreme, by supplying only the sound—

almost always a voice—and withholding the image of the sound's true source until nearly the very end of the film. Only then, when the audience has used its imagination to the fullest, as in a radio play, is the real identity of the source revealed, almost always with an accompanying loss of imagined power: the wizard in *The Wizard of Oz* is one of a number of examples cited, along with Hal in *2001* and the mother in *Psycho*. The Acousmêtre is, for various reasons having to do with our perceptions (the disembodied voice seems to come from everywhere and therefore to have no clearly defined limits to its power), a uniquely cinematic device. And yet . . .

And yet there is an echo here of our earliest experience of the world: the revelation at birth (or soon after) that the song that sang to us from the very dawn of our consciousness in the womb—a song that seemed to come from everywhere and to be part of us before we had any conception of what "us" meant— that this song is the voice of another and that she is now separate from us and we from her. We regret the loss of former unity— some say that our lives are a ceaseless quest to retrieve it—and yet we delight in seeing the face of our mother: the one is the price to be paid for the other.

This earliest, most powerful fusion of sound and image sets the tone for all that are to come. One of the dominant themes of my experience with sound, ever since that first encounter at age ten, has been continual discovery—the exhilaration forty years later of coming upon new features of a landscape that has still not been entirely mapped out. Chion's contributions here and in his previous books combine a serious attempt to discover the true coordinates and features of this continent of sound with the excitement of those early explorers who have forged their own path through the forests and return with tales of wonderful things seen for the

first time. For all that Chion pursues the goal of a coherent theory, though, perhaps his theory's greatest attribute is its recognition that within that coherence there is no place for completeness—that there will always be something about sound that
"bypasses and surprises us," and that we must never entirely succeed in taming the dancing shadow and the singing soul.

PREFACE

Theories of the cinema until now have tended to elude the issue of sound, either by completely ignoring it or by relegating it to minor status. Even if some scholars have made rich and provocative contributions here and there, their insights (including my own, in three previous books on the subject) have not yet been influential enough to bring about a total reconsideration of the cinema in light of the position that sound has occupied in it for the last sixty years.

And yet films, television, and other audiovisual media do not just address the eye. They place their spectators—their audio-spectators—in a specific perceptual mode of reception, which in this book I shall call *audio-vision*.

Oddly enough, the newness of this activity has received little consideration. In continuing to say that we "see" a film or a television program, we persist in ignoring how the soundtrack has modified perception. At best, some people are content with an additive model, according to which witnessing an audiovisual spectacle basically consists of seeing images plus hearing sounds. Each perception remains nicely in its own compartment.

The objective of this book is to demonstrate the reality of audiovisual combination—that one perception influences the other and transforms it. We never see the same thing when we also hear; we don't hear the same thing when we see as well. We must therefore get beyond preoccupations such as identifying so-called redundancy between the two domains and debating interrelations between forces (the famous question asked in the seventies, "Which is more important, sound or image?").

This work is at once theoretical and practical. First, it describes and formulates the audiovisual relationship as a contract—that is, as the opposite of a natural relationship arising from some sort of preexisting harmony among the perceptions. Then it outlines a method for observation and analysis that has developed from my teaching experience and may be applied to films, television programs, videos, and so forth. Since the perspective I offer here is new, it is my hope that the reader will forgive me for being neither definitive nor exhaustive.

I have already written three books on sound (*La Voix au cinéma*, *Le Son au cinéma*, and *La Toile trouée*, all published by *Cahiers du cinéma*). In the present volume the reader will find ideas proposed in those previous essays, but set in a wider conceptual framework, a more systematic presentation, and with many new refinements.

The chapters that make up part 1, "The Audiovisual Contract," sum up a series of possible "answers." The chapters that follow, under the general rubric "Beyond Sounds and Images," try to formulate the questions and to push beyond established barriers and compartmentalized perspectives. Film is my central concern, but I have also considered individual cases of television, video art, and music videos.

Since aural perception is the least understood and the least practiced, at the beginning of this book I have put forth certain tenets of theory of sound and hearing. For more details on these questions, the reader may refer to my *Guide des objets sonores*.

This work is indebted to my discussions and exchanges with students at IDHEC (Institut des hautes études cinématographiques), IDA (Audiovisual Studies Institute, Paris), DERCAV (the film department at the University of Paris III), INSAS (National Film School) in Brussels, the Paris Film and Critical Studies Center, the École des Arts in Lausanne, the Gen Lock association of Geneva, ACT in Toulouse, and the University of Iowa. I thank the prime movers and administrators of these centers. And for their constructive criticism, I am grateful to Christiane Sacco-Zagaroli, Rick Altman, Patrice Rollet, and, of course, Michel Marie, to whom this book owes its existence.

AUDIO-VISION

. . .

PART 1

. . .

THE
AUDIOVISUAL
CONTRACT

ONE

PROJECTIONS OF
SOUND ON IMAGE

. . .

The house lights go down and the movie begins. Brutal and enigmatic images appear on the screen: a film projector running, a closeup of the film going through it, terrifying glimpses of animal sacrifices, a nail being driven through a hand. Then, in more "normal" time, a mortuary. Here we see a young boy we take at first to be a corpse like the others, but who turns out to be alive—he moves, he reads a book, he reaches toward the screen surface, and under his hand there seems to form the face of a beautiful woman.

What we have seen so far is the prologue sequence of Bergman's *Persona*, a film that has been analyzed in books and university courses by the likes of Raymond Bellour, David Bordwell, Marilyn Johns Blackwell. And the film might go on this way.

Stop! Let us rewind Bergman's film to the beginning and simply *cut out the sound*, try to forget what we've seen before, and watch the film afresh. Now we see something quite different.

First, the shot of the nail impaling the hand: played silent, it turns out to have consisted of three separate shots where we had seen one, because they had been linked by sound. What's more, the nailed hand in silence is abstract, whereas with sound, it is terrifying, real. As for the shots in the mortuary, without the sound of dripping water that connected them together we discover in them a series of stills, parts of isolated human bodies, out of space and time. And the boy's right hand, without the vibrating tone that accompanies and structures its exploring gestures, no longer "forms" the face, but just wanders aimlessly. The entire sequence has lost its rhythm and unity. Could Bergman be an overrated director? Did the sound merely conceal the images' emptiness?

Next let us consider a well-known sequence in Tati's *Monsieur Hulot's Holiday*, where subtle gags on a small bathing beach make us laugh. The vacationers are so amusing in their uptightness, their lack of fun, their anxiety! This time, let's cut out the visuals. Surprise: like the flipside of the image, another film appears that we now "see" with only our ears; there are shouts of children having fun, voices that resonate in an outdoor space, a whole world of play and vitality. It was all there in the sound, and at the same time it wasn't.

Now if we give Bergman back his sounds and Tati his images, everything returns to normal. The nailed hand makes you sick to look at, the boy shapes his faces, the summer vacationers seem quaint and droll, and sounds we didn't especially hear when there was only sound emerge from the image like dialogue balloons in comics.

Only now we have read and heard in a different way.

Is the notion of cinema as the art of the image just an illusion? Of course: how, ultimately, can it be anything else? This book is about precisely this phenomenon of *audiovisual illusion*, an illusion located first and foremost in the heart of the most important of relations between sound and image, as illustrated above with Bergman: what we shall call *added value*.

By *added value* I mean the expressive and informative value with which a sound enriches a given image so as to create the definite impression, in the immediate or remembered experience one has of it, that this information or expression "naturally" comes from what is seen, and is already contained in the image itself. Added value is what gives the (eminently incorrect) impression that sound is unnecessary, that sound merely duplicates a meaning which in reality it brings about, either all on its own or by discrepancies between it and the image.

The phenomenon of added value is especially at work in the case of sound/image synchronism, via the principle of *synchresis* (see chapter 3), the forging of an immediate and necessary relationship between something one sees and something one hears. Most falls, blows, and explosions on the screen, simulated to some extent or created from the impact of nonresistant materials, only take on consistency and materiality through sound. But first, at the most basic level, added value is that of text, or language, on image.

Why speak of language so early on? Because the cinema is a vococentric or, more precisely, a verbocentric phenomenon.

Value Added by Text[1]

In stating that sound in the cinema is primarily vococentric, I mean that it almost always privileges the voice, highlighting and setting the latter off from other sounds. During filming it is the voice that is collected in sound recording—which therefore is almost always voice recording—and it is the voice that is isolated in the sound mix like a solo instrument—for which the other sounds (music and noise) are merely the accompaniment. By the same token, the historical development of synch sound recording technology, for example, the invention of new kinds of microphones and sound systems, has concentrated essentially on speech since of course we are not talking about the voice of shouts and moans, but the voice as medium of verbal expression. And in voice recording what is sought is not so much acoustical fidelity to original timbre, as the guarantee of effortless intelligibility of the words spoken. Thus what we mean by vococentrism is almost always verbocentrism.

Sound in film is voco- and verbocentric, above all, because human beings in their habitual behavior are as well. When in any given sound environment you hear voices, those voices capture and focus your attention before any other sound (wind blowing, music, traffic). Only afterward, if you know very well who is speaking and what they're talking about, might you turn your attention from the voices to the rest of the sounds you hear. So if these voices speak in an accessible language, you will first seek the meaning of the words, moving on to interpret the other sounds only when your interest in meaning has been satisfied.

Text Structures Vision

An eloquent example that I often draw on in my classes to demonstrate value added by text is a TV broadcast from 1984, a transmission of an air show in England, anchored from a French studio for French audiences by our own Léon Zitrone[2]. Visibly thrown by these images coming to him on the wire with no explanation and in no special order, the valiant anchor nevertheless does his job as well as he can. At a certain point, he affirms, "Here

are three small airplanes," as we see an image with, yes, three little airplanes against a blue sky, and the outrageous redundancy
never fails to provoke laughter.

Zitrone could just as well have said, "The weather is magnificent today," and that's what we would have seen in the image,
where there are in fact no clouds. Or: "The first two planes are
ahead of the third," and then everyone would have seen *that*. Or
else: "Where did the fourth plane go?"—and the fourth airplane's
absence, this plane hopping out of Zitrone's hat by the sheer
power of the Word, would have jumped to our eyes. In short, the
anchor could have made fifty other "redundant" comments; but
their redundancy is illusory, since in each case these statements
would have guided and structured our vision so that we would
have seen them "naturally" in the image.

The weakness of Chris Marker's famous demonstration in his
documentary *Letter from Siberia*—already critiqued by Pascal
Bonitzer in another context[3]—where Marker dubs voiceovers of
different political persuasions (Stalinist, anti-Stalinist, etc.) over
the same sequence of innocuous images, is that through his exag-
gerated examples he leads us to believe that the issue is solely one
of political ideology, and that otherwise there exists some neutral
way of speaking. The added value that words bring to the image
goes far beyond the simple situation of a political opinion slapped
onto images; added value engages the very structuring of vision—
by rigorously framing it. In any case, the evanescent film image
does not give us much time to look, unlike a painting on a wall or
a photograph in a book that we can explore at our own pace and
more easily detach from their captions or their commentary.

Thus if the film or TV image seems to "speak" for itself, it is
actually a ventriloquist's speech. When the shot of the three small
airplanes in a blue sky declares "three small airplanes," it is a
puppet animated by the anchorman's voice.

VALUE ADDED BY MUSIC

Empathetic and Anempathetic Effects

In my book *Le Son au cinéma* I developed the idea that there are two ways for music in film to create a specific emotion in relation to the situation depicted on the screen.[4] On one hand, music can directly express its participation in the feeling of the scene, by taking on the scene's rhythm, tone, and phrasing; obviously such music participates in cultural codes for things like sadness, happiness, and movement. In this case we can speak of *empathetic music*, from the word empathy, the ability to feel the feelings of others.

On the other hand, music can also exhibit conspicuous indifference to the situation, by progressing in a steady, undaunted, and ineluctable manner: the scene takes place against this very backdrop of "indifference." This juxtaposition of scene with indifferent music has the effect not of freezing emotion but rather of intensifying it, by inscribing it on a cosmic background. I call this second kind of music *anempathetic* (with the privative *a*-). The anempathetic impulse in the cinema produces those countless musical bits from player pianos, celestas, music boxes, and dance bands, whose studied frivolity and naiveté reinforce the individual emotion of the character and of the spectator, even as the music pretends not to notice them.

To be sure, this effect of cosmic indifference was already present in many operas, when emotional pitch was so high that it froze characters into inaction, provoking a sort of psychotic regression. Hence the famous operatic convention of madness, with the dumb little music that a character repeats while rocking back and forth. . . . But on the screen the anempathetic effect has taken on such prominence that we have reason to consider it to be intimately related to cinema's essence—its mechanical nature.

For, indeed, all films proceed in the form of an indifferent and automatic unwinding, that of the projection, which on the screen and through the loudspeakers produces simulacra of movement and life—and this unwinding must hide itself and be forgotten. What does anempathetic music do, if not to unveil this reality of cinema, its robotic face? Anempathetic music conjures up the mechanical texture of this tapestry of the emotions and senses.

Finally, there also exist cases of music that is neither empathetic nor anempathetic, which has either an abstract meaning, or a simple function of presence, a value as a signpost: at any rate, no precise emotional resonance.

The anempathetic effect is most often produced by music, but it can also occur with noise—when, for example, in a very violent scene after the death of a character some sonic process continues, like the noise of a machine, the hum of a fan, a shower running, as if nothing had happened. Examples of these can be found in Hitchcock's *Psycho* (the shower) and Antonioni's *The Passenger* (an electric fan).

INFLUENCES OF SOUND ON THE PERCEPTION OF MOVEMENT AND PERCEPTION OF SPEED

Visual and auditory perception are of much more disparate natures than one might think. The reason we are only dimly aware of this is that these two perceptions mutually influence each other in the audiovisual contract, lending each other their respective properties by contamination and projection.[5]

For one thing, each kind of perception bears a fundamentally different relationship to motion and stasis, since sound, contrary to sight, presupposes movement from the outset. In a film image that contains movement many other things in the frame may remain fixed. But sound by its very nature necessarily implies a displacement or agitation, however minimal. Sound does have means to suggest stasis, but only in limited cases. One could say that "fixed sound" is that which entails no variations whatever as it is heard. This characteristic is only found in certain sounds of artificial origin: a telephone dial tone, or the hum of a speaker. Torrents and waterfalls can produce a rumbling close to white noise too, but it is rare not to hear at least some trace of irregularity and motion. The effect of a fixed sound can also be created by taking a variation or evolution and infinitely repeating it in a loop. As the trace of a movement or a trajectory, sound thus has its own temporal dynamic.

Difference in Speed of Perception

Sound perception and visual perception have their own average pace by their very nature; basically, the ear analyzes, processes, and synthesizes faster than the eye. Take a rapid visual movement—a hand gesture—and compare it to an abrupt sound trajectory of the same duration. The fast visual movement will not form a distinct figure, its trajectory will not enter the memory in a precise picture. In the same length of time the sound trajectory will succeed in outlining a clear and definite form, individuated, recognizable, distinguishable from others.

This is not a matter of attention. We might watch the shot of visual movement ten times attentively (say, a character making a complicated arm gesture), and still not be able to discern its line clearly. Listen ten times to the rapid sound sequence, and your perception of it will be confirmed with more and more precision.

There are several reasons for this. First, for hearing individuals, sound is the vehicle of language, and a spoken sentence makes the ear work very quickly; by comparison, reading with the eyes is notably slower, except in specific cases of special training, as for deaf people. The eye perceives more slowly because it has more to do all at once; it must explore in space as well as follow along in time. The ear isolates a detail of its auditory field and it follows this point or line in time. (If the sound at hand is a familiar piece of music, however, the listener's auditory attention strays more easily from the temporal thread to explore spatially.) So, overall, in a first contact with an audiovisual message, the eye is more spatially adept, and the ear more temporally adept.

Sound for "Spotting" Visual Movements and for Sleight-of-Hand

In the course of audio-viewing a sound film, the spectator does not note these different speeds of cognition as such, because added value intervenes. Why, for example, don't the myriad rapid visual movements in kung fu or special effects movies create a confusing impression? The answer is that they are "spotted" by rapid auditory punctuation, in the form of whistles, shouts, bangs, and tinkling that mark certain moments and leave a strong audiovisual memory.

Silent films already had a certain predilection for rapid montages of events. But in its montage sequences the silent cinema was careful to simplify the image to the maximum; that is, it limited exploratory perception in space so as to facilitate perception in time. This meant a highly stylized visual mode analogous to rough sketches. Eisenstein's *The General Line* provides an excellent example with its closeups in the cream separator sequence.

If the sound cinema often has complex and fleeting movements issuing from the heart of a frame teeming with characters and other visual details, this is because the sound superimposed onto the image is capable of directing our attention to a particular visual trajectory. Sound even raises the possibility of sleight-of-hand effects: sometimes it succeeds in making us see in the image a rapid movement that isn't even there.

We find an eloquent example in the work of sound designer Ben Burtt on the *Star Wars* saga. Burtt had devised, as a sound effect for an automatic door opening (think of the hexagonal or diamond-shaped automatic doors of sci-fi films), a dynamic and convincing pneumatic "shhh" sound. So convincing, in fact, that, in making *The Empire Strikes Back*, when director Irving Kershner needed a door-closing effect he sometimes simply took a static shot of the closed door and followed it with a shot of the door open. As a result of sound editing, with Ben Burtt's "psssht," spectators who have nothing before their eyes besides a straight cut nevertheless think they see the door slide open. Added value is working full steam here, in accordance with a phenomenon specific to sound film that we might call faster-than-the-eye.

Deaf people raised on sign language apparently develop a special ability to read and structure rapid visual phenomena. This raises the question whether the deaf mobilize the same regions at the center of the brain as hearing people do for sound—one of the many phenomena that lead us to question received wisdom about distinctions between the categories of sound and image.

The Ear's Temporal Threshold

Further, we need to correct the formulation that hearing occurs in continuity. The ear in fact listens in brief slices, and what it perceives and remembers *already* consists in short syntheses of two or three seconds of the sound as it evolves. However, within these two or three seconds, which are perceived as a gestalt, the ear, or rather the ear-brain system, has minutely and seriously done its investigation such that its overall report of the event, delivered periodically, is crammed with the precise and specific data that have been gathered.

This results in a paradox: we don't hear sounds, in the sense of recognizing them, until shortly after we have perceived them. Clap your hands sharply and listen to the resulting sound. Hearing—namely the synthesized apprehension of a small fragment of the auditory event, consigned to memory—will *follow* the event very closely, it will not be totally simultaneous with it.

INFLUENCE OF SOUND ON THE PERCEPTION OF TIME IN THE IMAGE

Three Aspects of Temporalization

One of the most important effects of added value relates to the *perception of time in the image,* upon which sound can exert considerable influence. An extreme example, as we have seen, is found in the prologue sequence of *Persona,* where atemporal static shots are inscribed into a time continuum via the sounds of dripping water and footsteps. Sound temporalizes images in three ways.

The first is temporal animation of the image. To varying degrees, sound renders the perception of time in the image as exact, detailed, immediate, concrete—or vague, fluctuating, broad.

Second, sound endows shots with temporal linearization. In the silent cinema, shots do not always indicate temporal succession, wherein what happens in shot B would necessarily follow what is shown in shot A. But synchronous sound does impose a sense of succession.

Third, sound *vectorizes* or dramatizes shots, orienting them toward a future, a goal, and creation of a feeling of imminence and expectation. The shot is going somewhere and it is oriented in time. We can see this effect at work clearly in the prologue of *Persona*—in its first shot, for example.

Conditions Necessary for Sound to Temporalize Images

In order to function, these three effects depend on the nature of the sounds and images being put together.

First case: *the image has no temporal animation or vectorization in itself*. This is the case for a static shot, or one whose movement consists only of a general fluctuating, with no indication of possible resolution—for example, rippling water. In this instance, sound can bring the image into a temporality that it introduces entirely on its own.

Second case: *the image itself has temporal animation* (movement of characters or objects, movement of smoke or light, mobile framing). Here, sound's temporality *combines* with the temporality already present in the image. The two may move in concert or slightly at odds with each other, in the same manner as two instruments playing simultaneously.

Temporalization also depends on the type of sounds present. Depending on density, internal texture, tone quality, and progression, a sound can temporally animate an image to a greater or lesser degree, and with a more or less driving or restrained rhythm.[6] Different factors come into play here:

> 1. *How sound is sustained*. A smooth and continuous sound is less "animating" than an uneven or fluttering one. Try accompanying an image first with a prolonged steady note on the violin, and then with the same note played with a tremolo made by rapidly moving the bow. The second sound will cause a more tense and immediate focusing of attention on the image.

2. *How predictable the sound is as it progresses*. A sound with a regular pulse (such as a basso continuo in music or a mechanical ticking) is more predictable and tends to create less temporal animation than a sound that is irregular and thus unpredictable; the latter puts the ear and the attention on constant alert. The dripping of water in *Persona* as well as in Tarkovsky's films provide good examples: each unsettles our attention through its unequal rhythm.

However, a rhythm that is too regularly cyclical can also create an effect of tension, because the listener lies in wait for the possibility of a fluctuation in such mechanical regularity.

3. *Tempo*. How the soundtrack temporally animates the image is not simply a mechanical question of tempo. A rapid piece of music will not necessarily accelerate the perception of the image. Temporalization actually depends more on the regularity or irregularity of the aural flow than on tempo in the musical sense of the word. For example, if the flow of musical notes is unstable but moderate in speed, the temporal animation will be greater than if the speed is rapid but regular.

4. *Sound definition*. A sound rich in high frequencies will command perception more acutely; this explains why the spectator is on the alert in many recent films.

Temporalization also depends on the *model of sound-image linkage* and on the *distribution of synch points* (see below). Here, also, the extent to which sound activates an image depends on how it introduces points of synchronization—predictably or not, variously or monotonously. Control over expectations tends to play a powerful part in temporalization.

In summary, for sound to influence the image's temporality, a minimum number of conditions are necessary. First, the image must lend itself to it, either by being static and passively receptive (cf. the static shots of *Persona*) or by having a particular movement of its own (microrhythms "temporalizable" by sound). In the second case, the image should contain a minimum of structural elements—either elements of agreement, engagement, and sympathy (as we say of vibrations), or of active antipathy—with the flow of sound.

By visual *microrhythms* I mean rapid movements on the image's surface caused by things such as curls of smoke, rain, snowflakes, undulations of the rippled surface of a lake, dunes, and so forth—even the swarming movement of photographic grain itself, when visible. These phenomena create rapid and fluid rhythmic values, instilling a vibrating, trembling temporality in the image itself. Kurosawa utilizes them systematically in his film *Dreams* (petals raining down from flowering trees, fog, snowflakes in a blizzard). Hans-Jürgen Syberberg, in his static and posed long takes, also loves to inject visual microrhythms (smoke machines in *Hitler*, the flickering candle during Edith Clever's reading of Molly Bloom's monologue, etc.), as does Manoel de Oliveira (*Le Soulier de satin*). It is as if this technique affirms a kind of time proper to sound cinema as a recording of the microstructure of the present.

Sound Cinema is Chronography

One important historical point has tended to remain hidden: we are indebted to synchronous sound for having made cinema an art of time. The stabilization of projection speed, made necessary by the coming of sound, did have consequences that far surpassed what anyone could have foreseen. Filmic time was no longer a flexible value, more or less transposable depending on the rhythm of projection. Time henceforth had a fixed value; sound cinema guaranteed that whatever lasted x seconds in the editing would still have this same exact duration in the screening. In the silent cinema a shot had no exact internal duration; leaves quivering in the wind and ripples on the surface of the water had no absolute or fixed temporality. Each exhibitor had a certain margin of freedom in setting the rhythm of projection speed. Nor is it any accident that the motorized editing table, with its standardized film speed, did not appear until the sound era.

Note that I am speaking here of the rhythm of the finished film. Within a film there certainly may be material shot at nonstandard speeds—accelerated or slow-motion—as seen in works of Michael Powell, Scorsese, Peckinpah, or Fellini at different points in sound film history. But if the speed of these shots does not necessarily reproduce the real speed at which the actors moved during filming, it *is* fixed in any case at a precisely determined and controlled rate.

So sound temporalized the image: not only by the effect of added value but also quite simply by normalizing and stabilizing film projection speed. A silent film by Tarkovsky, who called cinema "the art of sculpting in time," would not be conceivable. His long takes are animated with rhythmic quiverings, convulsions, and fleeting apparitions that, in combination with vast controlled visual rhythms and movements, form a kind of hypersensitive temporal structure. The sound cinema can therefore be called "chronographic": written in time as well as in movement.

Temporal Linearization

When a sequence of images does not necessarily show temporal succession in the actions it depicts—that is, when we can read them equally as simultaneous or successive—the addition of realistic, diegetic sound imposes on the sequence a sense of real time, like normal everyday experience, and above all, a sense of time that is linear and sequential.

Let us take a scene that occurs frequently enough in silent film: a crowd reacting, constructed as a montage of closeups of scowling or grinning faces. Without sound the shots that follow one another on the screen need not designate actions that are temporally related. One can quite easily understand the reactions as being simultaneous, existing in a time analogous to the perfect tense in grammar. But if we dub onto these images the sounds of collective booing or laughter, they seem magically to fall into a linear time continuum. Shot B shows someone who laughs or jeers *after* the character in shot A.

The awkwardness of some crowd scenes in the very earliest talkies derives from this. For example, in the opening company dinner of Renoir's *La Chienne*, the sound (laughter, various verbal exchanges among the partygoers) seems to be stuck onto images that are conceived as inscribed in a kind of time that was not yet linear.

The sound of the spoken voice, at least when it is diegetic and synched with the image, has the power to inscribe the image in a real and linearized time that no longer has elasticity. This factor explains the dismay of many silent filmmakers upon experiencing the effect of "everyday time" at the coming of sound.

Synchresis, which we shall discuss at greater length in chapter 3, is a powerful factor in linearizing and inscribing images into real time.

Vectorization of Real Time

Imagine a peaceful shot in a film set in the tropics, where a woman is ensconced in a rocking chair on a veranda, dozing, her chest rising and falling regularly. The breeze stirs the curtains and the bamboo windchimes that hang by the doorway. The leaves of the banana trees flutter in the wind. We could take this poetic shot and easily project it from the last frame to the first, and this would change essentially nothing, it would all look just as natural. We can say that the time this shot depicts is real, since it is full of microevents that reconstitute the texture of the present, but that it is not vectorized. Between the sense of moving from past to future and future to past we cannot confirm a single noticeable difference.

Now let us take some sounds to go with the shot—direct sound recorded during filming, or a soundtrack mixed after the fact: the woman's breathing, the wind, the chinking of the bamboo chimes. If we now play the film in reverse, it no longer works at all, especially the windchimes. Why? Because each one of these clinking sounds, consisting of an attack and then a slight fading resonance, is a finite story, oriented in time in a precise and irreversible manner. Played in reverse, it can immediately be recognized as "backwards." Sounds are vectorized.

The same is true for the dripping water in the prologue of *Persona*. The sound of the smallest droplet imposes a real and irreversible time on what we see, in that it presents a trajectory in time (small impact, then delicate resonance) in accordance with logics of gravity and return to inertia.

This is the difference, in the cinema, between the orders of sound and image: given a comparable time scale (say two to three seconds), aural phenomena are much more characteristically vectorized in time, with an irreversible beginning, middle, and end, than are visual phenomena.

If this fact normally eludes us, it is because the cinema has derived amusement from exceptions and paradoxes by playing on what's visually irreversible: a broken object whose parts all fly back together, a demolished wall that reconstructs, or the inevitable gag of the swimmer coming out of the pool feet first and settling upon the diving board. Of course, images showing actions that result from nonreversible forces (gravity causes an object to fall, an explosion disperses fragments), is clearly vectorized. But much more frequently in movies, images of a character who speaks, smiles, plays the piano, or whatever are reversible; they are not marked with a sense of past and future. Sound, on the other hand, quite often consists of a marking off of small phenomena oriented in time. Isn't piano music, for example, composed of thousands of little indices of vectorized real time, since each note begins to die as soon as it is born?

Stridulation and Tremolo: Naturally or Culturally Based Influence

The temporal animation of the image by sound is not a purely physical and mechanical phenomenon: cinematic and cultural codes also play a part in it. A music cue or a voiceover that is culturally perceived as not "in" the setting will not set the image to vibrating. And yet, the phenomenon still has a noncultural basis.

Take the example of the string tremolo, a device traditionally employed in opera and symphonic music to create a feeling of dramatic tension, suspense, or alarm. In film we can get virtually the same result with sound effects: for example, the stridulation of nocturnal insects in the final scene of Randa Haines's *Children of a Lesser God*. This ambient sound, however, is not explicitly coded as a "tremolo"; it is not in the official repertoire of standard devices of filmic writing. Nevertheless it can have on the dramatic perception of time exactly the same effect of concentrating attention and making us sensitive to the smallest quivering on the screen, as does the tremolo in the orchestra. Sound editors and mixers frequently do utilize such nocturnal ambient sounds, and parcel out the effect like orchestra conductors, by their choices of certain sound-effects recordings and the ways they blend these to create an overall sound. Obviously the effect will vary according to the density of the stridulation, its regular or fluctuating quality, and its duration—just as for an orchestral effect.

But what exactly is there in common, for a film spectator, between a string tremolo in a pit orchestra, which the viewer identifies as a cultural musical procedure, and the rustling of an animal, which the viewer perceives as a natural emanation from the setting (without dreaming, of course, that the latter could have been recorded separately from the image and expertly recomposed)? Only an acoustic identity: that of a sharp, high, slightly uneven vibrating that both alarms and fascinates. It appears, then, that we have a universal and spontaneous effect operating here. It is also, however, a very fragile effect, which the slightest thing—bad sound balance, a spectator's loss of confidence in the audiovisual contract due to a fault in production—suffices to compromise.

This also holds true for all effects of added value that have nothing of the mechanical: founded on a psychophysiological basis, they operate only under certain cultural, aesthetic, and emotional conditions by means of a general interaction of all elements.

Reciprocity of Added Value: The Example of Sounds of Horror

Added value works reciprocally. Sound shows us the image differently than what the image shows alone, and the image likewise makes us hear sound differently than if the sound were ringing out in the dark. However for all this reciprocity the screen remains the principal support of filmic perception. Transformed by the image it influences, sound ultimately reprojects onto the image the product of their mutual influences. We find eloquent testimony to this reciprocity in the case of horrible or upsetting sounds. The image projects onto them a meaning they do not have at all by themselves.

Everyone knows that the classical sound film, which avoided showing certain things, called on sound to come to the rescue. Sound *suggested* the forbidden sight in a much more frightening way than if viewers were to see the spectacle with their own eyes. An archetypal example is found at the beginning of Aldrich's masterpiece, *Kiss Me Deadly*, when the runaway hitchhiker whom Ralph Meeker picked up has been recaptured by her pursuers and is being tortured. We see nothing of this torture but two bare legs kicking and struggling, while we hear the unfortunate woman's screams. There's a typical use of sound, we might say. Of course—as long as it's clear that what makes the screams so terrifying is not their own acoustic properties but what the narrated situation, and what we're allowed to see, project onto them.

Another traumatic aural effect occurs in a scene in *The Skin*, by Liliana Cavani (1981, based on Malaparte's novel). An American tank accidentally runs over a little Italian boy, with—if memory does not fail me—a ghastly noise that sounds like a watermelon being crushed. Although spectators are not likely to have heard the real sound of a human body in this circumstance, they may imagine that it has some of this humid, viscous quality. The sound here has obviously been Foleyed in, perhaps precisely by crushing a melon.

As we shall see, the figurative value of a sound in itself is usually quite nonspecific. Depending on the dramatic and visual context, a single sound can convey very diverse things. For the spectator, it is not acoustical realism so much as synchrony above all, and secondarily the factor of verisimilitude (verisimilitude arising not from truth but from convention), that will lead him or her to connect a sound with an event or detail. The same sound can convincingly serve as the sound effect for a crushed watermelon in a comedy or for a head blown to smithereens in a war film. The same noise will be joyful in one context, intolerable in another.

In Franju's *Eyes Without a Face* we find one of the rare disturbing sounds that the public and critics have actually remarked upon after viewing: the noise made by the body of a young woman—the hideous remains of an aborted skin-transplant experiment—when surgeon Pierre Brasseur and his accomplice Alida Valli drop it into a family vault. What this flat thud (which never fails to send a shudder through the theater) has in common with the noise in Cavani's film is that it transforms the human being into a thing, into vile, inert, disposable matter, with its entrails and osseous cavities.

But it is an upsetting noise also in that within the film's rhythm it constitutes an *interruption of speech*, a moment where the two perpetrators' speech is absent. At the cinema or in real life certain sounds have this resonance because they occur at a certain place: in a flow of language, where they make a hole. A ghastly example of this idea can be seen in Tarkovsky's *Andrei Rublov*. A Russian prince emerges from being tortured by the Tatars; he is covered with bandages, which hide his mutilated body and leave nothing visible but his lips. Abandoned on a bed, he curses his torturers; but just after, the torturer's hand brings a ladle full of boiling oil which is poured down his throat. This action is masked from view by the back of the torturer, who has mercifully (or rather cleverly) interposed himself at that moment between the spectator and the victim's head. What we hear is the atrocious sound of gargling, which makes the skin crawl. All the same, as with the crushing sound mentioned above, this could be the same sound Peter Sellers might make as he gargles in a Blake Edwards comedy.

Here, the effect of the sound is so strong because it represents human speech felled at its physical core: what has been destroyed are a larynx and a tongue, which have just spoken.

T W O

THE THREE

LISTENING MODES

. . .

CAUSAL LISTENING

When we ask someone to speak about what they have heard, their answers are striking for the heterogeneity of levels of hearing to which they refer. This is because there are at least three modes of listening, each of which addresses different objects.[1] We shall call them *causal listening, semantic listening,* and *reduced listening.*

Causal listening, the most common, consists of listening to a sound in order to gather information about its cause (or source). When the cause is visible, sound can provide supplementary information about it; for example, the sound produced by an enclosed container when you tap it indicates how full it is. When we cannot see the sound's cause, sound can constitute our principal source of information about it. An unseen cause might be identified by some knowledge or logical prognostication; causal listening (which rarely departs from zero) can elaborate on this knowledge.

We must take care not to overestimate the accuracy and potential of causal listening, its capacity to furnish sure, precise data solely on the basis of analyzing sound. In reality, causal listening is not only the most common but also the most easily influenced and deceptive mode of listening.

Identifying Causes: From the Unique to the General

Causal listening can take place on various levels. In some cases we can recognize the precise cause: a specific person's voice, the sound produced by a particular unique object. But we rarely recognize a unique source exclusively on the basis of sound we hear out of context. The human individual is probably the only cause that can produce a sound, the speaking voice, that characterizes that individual alone. Different dogs of the same species have the same bark. Or at least (and for most people it adds up to the same thing) we are not capable of distinguishing the barking of one bulldog from that of another bulldog or even a dog of a related breed. Even though dogs seem to be able to identify their master's voice from among hundreds of voices, it is quite doubtful that the master, with eyes closed and lacking further information, could similarly discern the voice of her or his own dog. What obscures this weakness in our causal listening is that when we're at home and hear barking in the back room, we can easily deduce that Fido or Rover is the responsible party.

At the same time, a source we might be closely acquainted with can go unidentified and unnamed indefinitely. We can listen to a radio announcer every day without having any idea of her name or her physical attributes. Which by no means prevents us from opening a file on this announcer in our memory, where vocal and personal details are noted, and where her name and other traits (hair color, facial features—to which her voice gives us no clue) remain blank for the time being. For there is a considerable difference between taking note of the individual's vocal timbre—and *identifying* her, having a visual image of her and committing it to memory and assigning her a name.

In another kind of causal listening we do not recognize an individual, or a unique and particular item, but rather a category of human, mechanical, or animal cause: an adult man's voice, a motorbike engine, the song of a meadowlark. Moreover, in still more ambiguous cases far more numerous than one might think, what we recognize is only the *general nature* of the sound's cause. We may say, "That must be something mechanical" (identified by a certain rhythm, a regularity aptly called "mechanical"); or, "That must be some animal" or "a human sound." For lack of anything more specific, we identify *indices*, particularly temporal ones, that we try to draw upon to discern the nature of the cause.

Even without identifying the source in the sense of the nature of the causal object, we can still follow with precision the *causal history* of the sound itself. For example, we can trace the evolution of a scraping noise (accelerating, rapid, slowing down, etc.) and sense changes in pressure, speed, and amplitude without having any idea of *what* is scraping against *what*.

The Source as a Rocket in Stages

Remember that a sound often has not just one source but at least two, three, even more. Take the sound of the felt-tip pen with which I am writing this draft. The sound's two main sources are the pen and the paper. But there are also the hand gestures involved in writing and, further, I who am writing. If this sound is recorded and listened to on a tape recorder, sound sources will also include the loudspeaker, the audio tape onto which the sound was recorded, and so forth.

Let us note that in the cinema, causal listening is constantly manipulated by the audiovisual contract itself, especially through the phenomenon of synchresis. Most of the time we are dealing not with the real initial causes of the sounds, but causes that the film makes us believe in.

SEMANTIC LISTENING

I call semantic listening that which refers to a code or a language to interpret a message: spoken language, of course, as well as Morse and other such codes. This mode of listening, which functions in an extremely complex way, has been the object of linguistic research and has been the most widely studied. One crucial finding is that it is purely differential. A phoneme is listened to not strictly for its acoustical properties but as part of an entire system of oppositions and differences. Thus semantic listening often ignores considerable differences in pronunciation (hence in sound) if they are not *pertinent* differences in the language in question. Linguistic listening in both French and English, for example, is not sensitive to some widely varying pronunciations of the phoneme *a*.

Obviously one can listen to a single sound sequence employing both the causal and semantic modes at once. We hear at once what someone says and how they say it. In a sense, causal listening to a voice is to listening to it semantically as perception of the handwriting of a written text is to reading it.[2]

REDUCED LISTENING

Pierre Schaeffer gave the name *reduced listening* to the listening mode that focuses on the traits of the sound itself, independent of its cause and of its meaning.[3] Reduced listening takes the sound—verbal, played on an instrument, noises, or whatever—as itself the object to be observed instead of as a vehicle for something else.

A session of reduced listening is quite an instructive experience. Participants quickly realize that in speaking about sounds they shuttle constantly between a sound's actual content, its source, and its meaning. They find out that it is no mean task to speak about sounds in themselves, if the listener is forced to describe them independently of any cause, meaning, or effect. And language we employ as a matter of habit suddenly reveals all its ambiguity: "This is a squeaky sound," you say, but in what sense? Is "squeaking" an image only, or is it rather a word that refers to a *source* that squeaks, or to an unpleasant *effect*?

So when faced with this difficulty of paying attention to sounds in themselves, people have certain reactions—"laughing off" the project, or identifying trivial or harebrained causes—which are in fact so many defenses. Others might avoid description by claiming to objectify sound via the aids of spectral analysis or stopwatches, but of course these machines only apprehend physical data, they do not designate what we hear. A third form of retreat involves entrenchment in out-and-out subjective relativism. According to this school of thought, every individual hears something different, and the sound perceived remains forever unknowable. But perception is not a purely individual phenomenon, since it partakes in a particular kind of objectivity, that of shared perceptions. And it is in this objectivity-born-of-intersubjectivity that reduced listening, as Schaeffer defined it, should be situated.

In reduced listening the descriptive inventory of a sound cannot be compiled in a single hearing. One has to listen many times over, and because of this the sound must be fixed, recorded. For a singer or a musician playing an instrument before you is unable to produce exactly the same sound each time. She or he can only reproduce its general pitch and outline, not the fine details that particularize a sound event and render it unique. Thus reduced listening requires the fixing of sounds, which thereby acquire the status of veritable objects.

Requirements of Reduced Listening

Reduced listening is an enterprise that is new, fruitful, and hardly natural. It disrupts established lazy habits and opens up a world of previously unimagined questions for those who try it. Everybody practices at least rudimentary forms of reduced listening. When we identify the pitch of a tone or figure out an interval between two notes, we are doing reduced listening; for pitch is an inherent characteristic of sound, independent of the sound's cause or the comprehension of its meaning.

What complicates matters is that a sound is not defined solely by its pitch; it has many other perceptual characteristics. Many common sounds do not even have a precise or determinate pitch; if they did, reduced listening would consist of nothing but good old traditional solfeggio practice. Can a descriptive system for sounds be formulated, independent of any consideration of their cause? Schaeffer showed this to be possible, but he only managed to stake out the territory, proposing, in his *Traité des objets musicaux*, a system of classification. This system is certainly neither complete nor immune to criticism, but it has the great merit of existing.

Indeed, it is impossible to develop such a system any further unless we create new concepts and criteria. Present everyday language as well as specialized musical terminology are totally inadequate to describe the sonic traits that are revealed when we practice reduced listening on recorded sounds.

In this book I am not about to go into great detail on reduced listening and sound description. The reader is encouraged to consult other books on this subject, particularly my own digest of Pierre Schaeffer's work published under the title of *Guide des objets sonores*.

What Is Reduced Listening Good For?

"What ultimately is the usefulness of reduced listening?" wondered the film and video students whom we obliged to immerse themselves in it for four days straight. Indeed, it would seem that film and television use sounds solely for their figurative, semantic, or evocatory value, in reference to real or suggested causes, or to texts—but only rarely as formal raw materials in themselves.

However, reduced listening has the enormous advantage of opening up our ears and sharpening our power of listening. Film and video makers, scholars, and technicians can get to know their medium better as a result of this experience and gain mastery over it. The emotional, physical, and aesthetic value of a sound is linked not only to the causal explanation we attribute to it but also to its own qualities of timbre and texture, to its own personal vibration. So just as directors and cinematographers—even those who will never make abstract films—have everything to gain by refining their knowledge of visual materials and textures, we can similarly benefit from disciplined attention to the inherent qualities of sounds.

The Acousmatic Dimension and Reduced Listening

Reduced listening and the acousmatic situation share something in common, but in a more ambiguous way than Pierre Schaeffer (who first developed both notions) gave us to understand. Schaeffer emphasized how acousmatic listening, which we shall define further on as a situation wherein one hears the sound without seeing its cause, can modify our listening. Acousmatic sound draws our attention to sound traits normally hidden from us by the simultaneous sight of the causes—hidden because this sight reinforces the perception of certain elements of the sound and obscures others. The acousmatic truly allows sound to reveal itself in all its dimensions.

At the same time, Schaeffer thought the acousmatic situation could encourage reduced listening, in that it provokes one to separate oneself from causes or effects in favor of consciously attending to sonic textures, masses, and velocities. But, on the contrary, the opposite often occurs, at least at first, since the acousmatic situation intensifies causal listening in taking away the aid of sight. Confronted with a sound from a loudspeaker that is presenting itself without a visual calling card, the listener is led all the more intently to ask, "What's that?" (i.e., "What is causing this sound?") and to be attuned to the minutest clues (often interpreted wrong anyway) that might help to identify the cause.[4]

When we listen acousmatically to recorded sounds it takes repeated hearings of a single sound to allow us gradually to stop attending to its cause and to more accurately perceive its own inherent traits.

A seasoned auditor can exercise causal listening and reduced listening in tandem, especially when the two are correlated. Indeed, what leads us to deduce a sound's cause if not the characteristic form it takes? Knowing that this is "the sound of x" allows us to proceed without further interference to explore what the sound is like in and of itself.

ACTIVE AND PASSIVE PERCEPTION

It seemed important, in the context of this book on audio-vision, to draw clear distinctions among the three modes of listening. But we must also remember that these three listening modes overlap and combine in the complex and varied context of the film soundtrack.

The question of listening with the ear is inseparable from that of listening with the mind, just as looking is with seeing. In other words, in order to describe perceptual phenomena, we must take into account that conscious and active perception is only one part of a wider perceptual field in operation. In the cinema to look is to explore, at once spatially and temporally, in a "given-to-see" (field of vision) that has limits contained by the screen. But listening, for its part, explores in a field of audition that is given or even imposed on the ear; this aural field is much less limited or confined, its contours uncertain and changing.

Due to natural factors of which we are all aware—the absence of anything like eyelids for the ears, the omnidirectionality of hearing, and the physical nature of sound—but also owing to a lack of any real aural training in our culture, this "imposed-to-hear" makes it exceedingly difficult for us to select or cut things out. There is always something about sound that overwhelms and surprises us no matter what—especially when we refuse to lend it our conscious attention; and thus sound interferes with our perception, affects it. Surely, our conscious perception can valiantly work at submitting everything to its control, but, in the present cultural state of things, sound more than image has the ability to saturate and short-circuit our perception.

The consequence for film is that sound, much more than the image, can become an insidious means of affective and semantic manipulation. On one hand, sound works on us directly, physiologically (breathing noises in a film can directly affect our own respiration). On the other, sound has an influence on perception: through the phenomenon of added value, it interprets the meaning of the image, and makes us see in the image what we would not otherwise see, or would see differently. And so we see that sound is not at all invested and localized in the same way as the image.

THREE

LINES AND POINTS: HORIZONTAL AND VERTICAL PERSPECTIVES ON AUDIOVISUAL RELATIONS

. . .

Harmony or Counterpoint?

The arrival of sound in the late twenties coincided with an extraordinary surge of aestheticism in silent film, and people took passionate interest in comparing cinema with music. This is why they came up with the term *counterpoint* to designate their notion of the sound film's ideal state as a cinema free of redundancy where sound and image would constitute two parallel and loosely connected tracks, neither dependent on the other.

Remember that in the language of Western classical music counterpoint refers to the mode of composition that conceives of each of several concurrent musical voices as individuated and coherent in its horizontal dimension. *Harmony* concerns the vertical dimension, and involves the relations of each note to the other notes heard at the same moment, together forming chords; harmony governs the conduct of the voices in the way these vertical chords are obtained. Training in classical composition involves learning both disciplines; and most musical works in the Western classical tradition combine these two dimensions, which are closely associated, to varying degrees.

If there exists something one can call audiovisual counterpoint, it occurs under conditions quite different from musical counterpoint. The latter exclusively uses notes—all the same raw material—while sound and image fall into different sensory categories. If there's any sense at all to the analogy, audiovisual counterpoint implies an "auditory voice" perceived horizontally in tandem with the visual track, a voice that possesses its own formal individuality.

What I wish to show is that films tend to exclude the possibility of such horizontal-contrapuntal dynamics. Quite to the contrary: in the cinema, harmonic and vertical relations (whether they be consonant, dissonant, or neither, à la Debussy) are generally more salient—i.e., the relations between a given sound and what is happening at that moment in the image. So to speak about counterpoint in the cinema is therefore to borrow a notion somewhat wrongheadedly, applying an intellectual speculation rather than a workable concept.

As proof we might note that historically, film studies quickly became muddled by this analogy, often to the point of using it entirely the wrong way. Many cases being offered up as models of counterpoint were actually splendid examples of *dissonant harmony*, since they point to a momentary discord between the image's and sound's figural natures. If we, too, sometimes make use of the musical analogy, we need to be careful: the term harmony doesn't take into account the specificity of audiovisual phenomena either.[1]

Our investigation of the horizontal and vertical aspects of the audiovisual sequence, to which this chapter is devoted, underscores their interdependence and their dialectical relationship. For instance, films characterized by a sort of horizontal freedom—the typical example is the music video, whose parallel image and sound tracks often have no precise relation—also exhibit a vigorous perceptual solidarity, marked by points of synchronization that occur throughout. These synch points—to return to the musical analogy—provide the harmonic framework of the audiovisual system.

Audiovisual Dissonance

Audiovisual counterpoint, which film aestheticians seem perennially to advocate, plead for, and insist upon, occurs on television every day, even though no one seems to notice. You can find it especially in replays of sports events, when the image goes its own way and the commentary goes another. I like to use the example of the coverage of a certain bicycle race in Barcelona. The image shows the racers from a helicopter. The soundtrack consists of a dialogue between the TV reporters and some cyclists not participating in the race. It is obvious that those speaking are not watching the images, nor are they saying anything remotely about them. Image and sound follow two totally different tracks for two minutes; the only thing giving any sense to the cohabitation of these two universes is the topic of cycling. And yet no one who views this clip notices its obvious counterpoint.

Why not? It is not enough if the sound and image differ in nature (the content of each, their spatial characteristics, etc.). Audiovisual counterpoint will be noticed only if it sets up an opposition between sound and image on a precise point of meaning. This kind of counterpoint influences our reading, in postulating a certain linear interpretation of the meaning of the sounds. Take for example the moment in Godard's *First Name Carmen* when we see the Paris metro and hear the cries of seagulls. Critics identified this as counterpoint, because the seagulls were considered as signifiers of "seashore setting" and the metro image as a signifier of "urban setting." This is what I mean by a linear interpretation: it reduces the audio and visual elements to abstractions at the expense of their multiple concrete particularities, which are much richer and full of ambiguity. Thus this counterpoint reduces our reading to a stereotyped meaning of the sounds, drawing on their *codedness* (seagulls = seashore) rather than their own sonic substance, their specific characteristics in the passage in question.

So the problem of counterpoint-as-contradiction, or rather of audiovisual dissonance, as it has been used and touted in films like Robbe-Grillet's *L'Homme qui ment*, is that counterpoint or dissonance implies a prereading of the relation between sound and image. By this I mean that it forces us to attribute simple, one-way meanings, since it is based on an opposition of a rhetorical nature ("I should hear X, but I hear Y"). In effect it imposes the model of language and its abstract categories, handled in yes-no, redundant-contradictory oppositions.

There exist hundreds of possible ways to add sound to any given image. Of this vast array of choices some are wholly conventional. Others, without formally contradicting or "negating" the image, carry the perception of the image to another level. And audiovisual dissonance is merely the inverse of convention, and thus pays homage to it, imprisoning us in a binary logic that has only remotely to do with how cinema works.

For an example of true *free counterpoint* consider the amazing resurrection scene in Tarkovsky's film *Solaris*. The hero's former wife, who committed suicide, comes back to him in flesh and blood on a space station, thanks to mysterious forces summoned forth by a brain-planet. Driven to despair on realizing that she is a nonhuman artifact, she kills herself yet again by swallowing liquid oxygen. The hero embraces her frozen body. But pitilessly the ocean-brain resuscitates her, and we see her body shaken with convulsions that are no longer those of agony or pleasure but of returning to "life." Over these images Tarkovsky had the imagination to dub sounds of breaking glass, which yield a phenomenal effect. We do not hear them as "wrong" or inappropriate sounds. Instead, they suggest that she is constituted of shards of ice; in a troubling, even terrifying way, they render both the creature's fragility and artificiality, and a sense of the precariousness of bodies.

The Predominance of the Vertical (There Is No Soundtrack)

In *La Voix au cinéma* I declared my position on the question of sound in the cinema, stating what ought to be obvious—that there is no soundtrack.[2]

Of course, no one would deny that in the purely technical sense of the word there does exist a sound channel that runs the length of the film. But this does not necessarily mean that the sounds of the film constitute a coherent entity.

If I do occasionally use the term *soundtrack* it is in a technical way, to designate empirically the simple end-to-end aggregation of all sounds in a film—inert and with no active autonomous meaning. In current parlance the idea of the soundtrack derives from a purely mechanical analogy with the image track; the latter is indeed a valid concept. The image track owes its being and its unity to the presence of a frame, a space of the images in which the spectator is invested.

By stating that *there is no soundtrack* I mean first of all that the sounds of a film, taken separately from the image, do not form an internally coherent entity on equal footing with the image track. Second, I mean that each audio element enters into *simultaneous vertical relationship* with narrative elements contained in the image (characters, actions) and visual elements of texture and setting. These relationships are much more direct and salient than any relations the audio element could have with other sounds. It's like a recipe: even if you mix the audio ingredients separately before pouring them into the image, a chemical reaction will occur to separate out the sounds and make each react on its own with the field of vision.

In the simplest and strongest relation, that of *offscreen sound*, the confrontation of sound with image establishes the sound as being offscreen, even as this sound is heard coming from the surface of the screen. Take away the image, and the offscreen sounds that were perceived apart from other sounds, purely by virtue of the visual exclusion of their source, become just like the others. The audiovisual structure collapses, and the sounds make a completely new one together. A film deprived of its image and transformed into an audio track proves altogether strange—provided you *listen* and refrain from imposing the images from your memory onto the sounds you hear. Only at this point can we talk about a soundtrack.

Therefore, there is no image track and no soundtrack in the cinema, but a *place* of images, plus sounds.

SOUND AND IMAGE IN RELATION TO EDITING

Sound Editing Has Not Created a Specific Unit

Sounds, like film images, are editable. By this I mean that they are recorded on strips of tape or film that can be cut, assembled, and moved around at will.

For the image it is this very fact of editing-construction that created the specific unit of cinema, the shot. The shot is a unit of greater or lesser pertinence for film analysis (depending on who has made the film and how), but is nevertheless quite convenient for doing breakdowns of films. Even if we do not consider shot 67 to be a structural narrative unit in itself but "only" a shot, i.e., the length of film between two splices, it is a great help to be able to say that the interesting, pertinent, significant element we are discussing can be found between the middle of shot 66 and the end of shot 68. The shot has the enormous advantage of being a neutral unit, objectively defined, that everyone who has made the film as well as those who watch it can agree on.

We can instantly see that no such condition obtains for sound: the editing of film sounds has created no specific sound unit. Unlike visual cuts, sound splices neither jump to our ears nor permit us to demarcate identifiable units of sound montage.

The cinema isn't the only place this occurs. Sounds have been edited since it became technically possible in radio (about sixty years ago) and in phonograph and tape recording. In none of these instances, regardless of whether images are involved, has the notion of an "auditory shot" or unit of sound montage emerged as a neutral, universally recognizable unit.

Possibility of Inaudible Sound Editing

On one hand, as we know, a film's "soundtrack" often consists of several layers independently recorded and mixed, which then overlap one another. Imagine a film resulting from mixing three layers of images in superimposition: only with great difficulty could one locate cuts. (This is the case in certain moments of Gance's *Napoleon* and Vertov's *Man with a Movie Camera*.)

On the other hand, the very nature of recorded sound events allows us to join one recorded sound with another in editing without the join being noticed. A film dialogue can be crawling with inaudible splices, impossible for the listener to detect. While, as we know, it is very difficult to invisibly join two shots filmed at different times—the cut jumps to our eyes. (Hitchcock made *Rope* look like a "one-shot film" by a simple trick, shooting the back of a character or a dark piece of furniture, so darkness fills the frame at the end and beginning of each reel.) Also, of course, auditory cuts can be quite distinctly heard. So both audible and inaudible editing are possible with sound.

In current practice the mixing of soundtracks consists essentially in the art of smoothing rough edges by degrees of intensity. This fact in itself already makes it impossible to adopt any unit of sound editing as a unit of perception or as a unit of film language.

However, some people view current practices not as "natural" but as the embodiment of a particular ideological and aesthetic position characteristic of the dominant cinema, conforming to the desire to bury the traces of work in order to give the film an appearance of continuity and transparency. Many analyses of this sort appeared in the sixties and seventies, invariably concluding with the call for a cinema of demystification based on discontinuity. Very few directors actually answered the call except Godard. Godard was one of the rare filmmakers to cut sounds as well as images, thereby accentuating jumps and discontinuities, in greatly restricting inaudible editing with its gradations of intensity and all the fades, dissolves, and other transitions always employed in editing sound in film.

Does an Audible Slice of Sound Make a "Sound Shot"?

Godard unmasks conventional sound editing all the more in the way he avoids the usual practice of mixing many tracks at once such that our attention is not grabbed by breaks and cuts in the sonic flow—in some of his films he limits the tracks to two. The result is that our attention can follow the thread of the sonic discourse, and it can hear unadorned all the ruptures, since the latter are made audible. Godard's films set up the most frank and radical conditions to apprehend what could be called a sound shot.

For example, in the beginning of *Hail Mary* (*Je vous salue Marie*) we can plainly hear the cuts that demarcate the slices of sound: a fragment of a Bach prelude played on a piano, shouts of a women's basketball team playing in a gym, offscreen voices, and so forth. For the listener, however, these perfectly demarcated sound slices do not add up to create a sense of units. Sound perception, which always occurs in time, merely jumps across the obstacle of the cut and then moves on to something else, forgetting the form of what it heard just before. The sound segment, especially if it lasts any time at all, does not synthesize into any particular bloc or totality in our perception.

Note that the same holds true for visual shots when they involve constantly mobile framing. Vision under these conditions occurs more along the flow of time, since it has no stable spatial referent. In the case of a sequence composed of static (or less constantly moving) shots, we can identify each shot by a certain composition, mise-en-scène, and perspective, and so we find it easy to represent this spatial arrangement in our memory.

On the other hand—even in the case of a stable sonic background cut up into little fragments as by Godard—it is inevitably sequential, temporal perception that still dominates for sound, at least for sounds of some duration.

And, above all, you cannot create an abstract and structural relationship between two successive sound segments (e.g., a fragment of bird calls or of music) the way you can between shots (a character looks offscreen—cut to what he is looking at; or an establishing shot—cut to a detail in the scene). If you try something like this with the soundtrack, the abstract relation you wish to establish gets drowned in the temporal flow. What strikes the listener instead is the dynamics of the break itself between the two fragments. The explanation of this mystery is that when we talk about a shot we are lumping together the shot's space and its duration, its spatial surface and its temporal dimension. While for sound pieces the temporal dimension seems to predominate, and the spatial dimension not to exist at all.

So that when the audiovisual contract is in force, governing the copresence of visual and auditory channels, visual cuts continue to provide the reference point for perception. If Godard's sound cuts "fracture" the shot's continuity, as some scholars poetically put it, they're hardly creating more than a hairline crack in a glass pane that remains essentially intact.

Necessary Conditions for a Place of Sounds

The example of *Hail Mary* is interesting for additional reasons. Godard imposed the rule not to use more than two audio tracks at any given time, as a personal constraint on himself; but the spectator is not thereby automatically aware of the two separate tracks. In fact, the only way really to notice these two tracks would be to assign each one to a different spatial source in the theater. With each attached to its own loudspeaker one would get the feeling of a real *place of the sound*, of a sonic container of sounds. Not only would the sounds have to issue from a source clearly distinct from the auditory space of the screen but in addition they would have to avoid any synchronizing with the visuals in order not to fall prey to the effect of spatial magnetization by the image (see chapter 4), which is generally the stronger!

Units, But Not Specific Ones

Does this mean that a film's soundtrack constitutes a continuous flow without breaks for the listener? Not at all, for we can still discern units. But such units—sentences, noises, musical themes, "cells" of sound—are exactly of the same type as in everyday experience, and we identify them according to criteria specific to the different types of sounds heard. If the scene has *dialogue*, our hearing analyzes the vocal flow into sentences, words—hence, linguistic units. Our perceptual breakdown of *noises* will proceed by distinguishing sound events, the more easily if there are isolated sounds. For a piece of *music* we identify the melodies, themes, and units of rhythmic patterns, to the extent that our musical training permits. In other words, we hear as usual, in units not specific to cinema that depend entirely on the type of sound and the chosen level of listening (semantic, causal, reduced).

The same thing obtains if we are obliged to separate out sounds in their *superimposition* and not in their succession. In order to do so we draw on a multitude of indices and levels of listening: differentiating masses and acoustic qualities, doing causal listening, and so on.

This explains why the specifically cinematic visual unit of the shot remains by far the most salient, and why the composition of the soundtrack is subordinate to the shot.

Sonic Flow: Internal Logic and External Logic

The flow of a film's sound is characterized by how well related, how fluidly or imperceptibly connected the various sound elements are, and whether they are successive and superimposed—or on the contrary, whether they have degrees of discontinuity, and are punctuated by breaks that interrupt one sound suddenly with another.

The spectator's general impression of sonic flow will result not from characteristics of editing and mixing conceived separately but from all the elements combined. Jacques Tati, for example, uses extremely pointed sound effects, recorded separately and inserted into the soundtrack's continuum at specific places. Heard in succession, they would make for a halting and fragmented soundtrack if not for his use of continuous background sounds to tie the whole thing together. Think for example of his "phantom" background voices (playing on the beach in *Mr. Hulot's Holiday*, hawking goods in the market in *Mon Oncle*), which act as connective tissue, nicely concealing the breaks that inevitably occur when one constructs an extremely fragmentary and discontinuous soundtrack.

I shall call *internal logic* of the audiovisual flow a mode of connecting images and sounds that appears to follow a flexible, organic process of development, variation, and growth, born out of the narrative situation itself and the feelings it inspires. Internal logic tends toward continuous and progressive modifications in the sonic flow, and makes use of sudden breaks only when the narrative so requires. I shall call *external logic* that which brings out effects of discontinuity and rupture as interventions external to the represented content: editing that disrupts the continuity of an image or a sound, breaks, interruptions, sudden changes of tempo, and so on.

Films like Ophuls's *Earrings of Madame de*, Fellini's *La Dolce Vita*, or Randa Haines's *Children of a Lesser God* adopt an internal logic. The sound swells, dies, reappears, diminishes, or grows as if cued by the characters' feelings, perceptions, or behaviors. Films such as Scott's *Alien*, Lang's *M*, or Godard's *Nouvelle Vague* obey an external logic, with marked effects of transitions and breaks.

Using external logic does not necessarily mean achieving critical distanciation—as critics often propose with regard to

Godard. In *Alien*, for example, the frequent jolts to sound continuity and the jerky progression of the visual and sound tracks—
characteristic of external logic—serve to reinforce the tension of
the action. It is true that in this case we have a science fiction film
where audio transmission by radio and phone, with their unpredictable fading in and out, is itself present as a concrete element
in the screenplay, and directly motivates many of these effects.
(For example, we see characters throw switches, turn on video
screens and work at control panels, thereby acting as manipula-
tors of sounds and images themselves.) Generally speaking, the
modern action-adventure film engages external logic quite
often.

But in a contemplative film like *The Goalie's Anxiety at the Penal-
ty Kick* by Wenders, sound as well as image use external logic in
response to a wholly different "literary" impulse, involving an
existential fragmentation into "impressions," little sensory
haikus.

SOUND IN THE AUDIOVISUAL CHAIN

Unification

The most widespread function of film sound consists of unifying
or binding the flow of images. First, in temporal terms, it unifies
by bridging the visual breaks through sound overlaps. Second, it
brings unity by establishing atmosphere (e.g., birdsongs or traffic
sounds) as a framework that seems to contain the image, a "heard
space" in which the "seen" bathes. And third, sound can provide
unity through nondiegetic music: because this music is independent of the notion of real time and space it can cast the images into
a homogenizing bath or current.

This function of the unifying sound bath, where sound temporally and spatially overflows the limits of shots on the screen,

has come under attack by what one might call the differential-ist school of criticism, which favors the idea of sound and image working in separate zones. Strangely, this approach neglects to criticize the same impulse toward unity when it is applied to the *image*. I am referring to the pursuit of visual continuity that prevails for cinematography in almost all films, whether silent or sound (including the films of Godard, Duras, and Syberberg), and that takes great pains with matching and balance of light and of color to make a well coordinated whole. Upon seeing a film consisting of four hundred to five hundred shots, would we be ready to perceive it as a succession of five hundred perfectly distinct units, as some experimental film-makers have attempted?

Punctuation

The function of punctuation in its widest grammatical sense (placement of commas, semicolons, periods, exclamation points, question marks, and ellipses, which can not only modulate the meaning and rhythm of a text but actually determine it as well), has long been a central concern of theater directing. The play's text is approached as a sort of continuum to be punctuated with bits of stage business already indicated to some degree by the stage directions but also worked out during rehearsal: pauses, intonation, breathing, gestures, and the like.

The silent cinema adopted the traditional methods of punctu-ating scenes and dialogues (for the cinema did, after all, have dia-logues). And it also naturally borrowed narrative techniques from opera, which used a great many punctuative musical effects by drawing on all the resources of the orchestra.

The silent cinema had multiple modes of punctuation: gestural, visual, and rhythmical. Intertitles functioned as a new and specific kind of punctuation as well. Beyond the printed text, the graphics of intertitles, the possibility of repeating them, and their interaction with the shots constituted so many means of inflecting the film.

So synchronous sound brought to the cinema not the *principle* of punctuation but increasingly subtle means of punctuating scenes without putting a strain on the acting or the editing. The barking of a dog offscreen, a grandfather clock ringing on the set, or a nearby piano are unobtrusive ways to emphasize a word, scan a dialogue, close a scene.

Punctuative use of sound depends on the initiative of the editor or the sound editor. They make decisions on the placement of sound punctuation based on the shot's rhythm, the acting, and the general feel of the scene, working with the sounds imposed on them or chosen by them. (In rare cases, the director makes such decisions him or herself, and some sound punctuation is already determined at the screenwriting stage.)

Naturally, music can play a major punctuative role. It certainly did in the silent era, but in a less precise, more approximate way, owing to the much looser methods of synchronizing music with image. And so it is not very surprising if certain early sound films dared to employ music in an unabashedly punctuative manner. John Ford's *The Informer*, with its score by Max Steiner, provides a good example.

Music as Symbolic Punctuation: *The Informer*

Hailed as an event in the film world on its release in 1935, John Ford's *Informer* appeared for many years on numerous Best Ten lists of all-time greatest films. Today, Fordians no longer tend to pay much attention to it at all. Its expressionism jars with the serenity and loftiness of vision they normally associate with their favorite director. However, despite the way it has aged (its principal weakness resides in the writing and performances of the female parts), it remains a very strong work.

Curiously enough, *The Informer* does not hold its place in film history so much for its own merits as for the legendary story of some gulps of beer.

Not only in the West—to paraphrase a line from *The Man Who Shot Liberty Valance*—do they print the legend when it is more popular than reality; it's the same everywhere. How are legends born? Out of a lack, a void that needs filling. Legends get going only when room has been made for them.

The same goes for the anecdote, often cited as the height of ridiculousness in film music aesthetics, about a drinker's swallowing that *The Informer*'s composer, in a frenzy of mickeymousing, went as far as to imitate musically. As early as 1937 we find the composer Maurice Jaubert claiming in a frequently quoted article: "In *The Informer*, the technique [of synchronism] is carried to its highest point of perfection, in the cue which is supposed to imitate the sound of coins falling to the ground, and even—with a suggestive little arpeggio—the trickling of a glass of beer down the gullet of a drinker."[3]

We can trace the lineage of this story through books on film music—including my own *Le Son au cinéma*, where, not having yet seen the film, I followed tradition and passed it on (which one should never do).[4] But when Ford's biographer Tag Gallagher tells the same anecdote and uses almost the same words ("beer gurgling in a man's throat"), I doubt whether he too is indebted to Jaubert. We are witness here to the spontaneous formation of a legend.

The reality that can be verified by watching a tape of the movie is that there is indeed a moment during which the protagonist is drinking, accompanied by a musical theme. But, first, it's a glass of whiskey and, second, the music at that moment couldn't be less imitative. Far from being a so-called suggestive little descending arpeggio, it is actually a resolute melody played on a solo French horn, ending with an upward jump of a diminished fifth, conveying something at once heroic and interrogative. It just can't be taken for gurgling. In fact the viewer recognizes it as one of the score's main themes—it is the first five notes of Gypo's theme, which has already been heard during the opening credits music. This motif accompanies the hero and is wed to his fate throughout the film, in an expressive way more than an imitative one.

Max Steiner based his *Informer* music on a principle that would subsequently dominate nine out of ten film scores—the principle of the leitmotif. Each main character or key thematic idea of the narrative is assigned a musical theme, which characterizes the character or idea and acts as its musical guardian angel. In *The Informer* the principal themes belong to Gypo (expressively rather neutral, and rather energetic and *marcato*, evoking Irish popular song) and to Katie, the prostitute-with-a-heart-of-gold whom Gypo loves (*espressivo* and *legato*). Then there is a special motif for the symbolic character of the Blind Man (a plaintive melody evoking the formal indeterminacy of Debussy). These musical themes are heard frequently in the orchestral score as "their" characters appear; they undergo changes that reflect variations in the characters' external circumstances and internal states. The theorizing and systematizing of the leitmotif of course goes back to Wagner, but if there is one opera in particular that inspired Steiner for *The Informer*, it must be Debussy's *Pelléas et Mélisande*. Despite his own caustic denunciation of leitmotif technique, Debussy used it himself, trying to make it more subtle by using more laconic, less pompous themes. Other Debussyesque touches in *The Informer* (as we shall see below) are an insistence on silences and a penchant for interruptions—when music halts and speech interposes itself into the vacuum.

The tendency here is to try to make a sound film into spoken opera, and in this endeavor we can see the hand of John Ford as well as that of the composer. *The Informer* certainly is not the kind of film that a composer was unleashed to slap a coat of musical paint onto after the shooting. The director, set designer, and composer worked together from the start, and judging from their own words, their preliminary consultations were much more extensive than is usual. Therefore, not only did Ford go along with the musical choices made for *The Informer* but he gave them his stamp of approval, perhaps even made his own suggestions.

The cornerstone of *The Informer*'s style is a predilection for stylization and symbolic expression—at the heart of a cinema that had just suffered the assaults of naturalism upon the coming of sound. This stylization obviously seeks to recapture the spirit of the silent film, perhaps even to achieve what the silent film could only dream of. The orchestra's punctuation of gestures and dialogue aims to undermine their purely realist and concrete aspects in favor of making them into signifying elements in an overall mise-en-scène.

In fact, Max Steiner's score hardly ever imitates the immediate materiality of the events; at least it does so much less than the great majority of film scores past and present. It does not emphasize the sounds of the elements, doors closing or bodies falling, and when it is heard with a particular movement on screen, its contours carefully *avoid* imitating the visual movement's form. Consider for example the scene to which Jaubert alludes from memory.

Let us recall that Gypo, the brutish outcast, has just turned in his friend Frankie, an Irish independence fighter wanted by the police, and he has gotten the reward money. He soon finds out that Frankie was killed on arrest. When he enters a bar, orders a whiskey, and raises his head to drink, it's because he is trying to forget. Gypo's musical theme plays at this moment, suggesting that even in his absence-to-himself, his identity insistently hangs on. Gypo, the grieving partner in the couple he formed with Frankie—who treated him with affectionate condescendence, as if he were the brain and Gypo the body—the incomplete Gypo, will find himself only by sacrificing himself, and the film tells the story of his coming to consciousness.

Already in Wagner's work there are themes in the orchestral fabric that embody a character's unconscious, giving voice to what the character does not know about himself. For example, in the first act of the *Walkyrie*, there is the sword motif, which (through the orchestra) works on Siegmund's unconscious, even before he finds the weapon in the hut where he has taken refuge. The barroom scene in *The Informer* also seems replete with a sense of meditation, of the stirring of dark things, and of preparation. It conveys something quite similar to Wagner's opening act, which has a very fragmented and discontinuous musical fabric that includes stops, reprises, and silences.

When the barkeeper returns the change to Gypo, four instrumental notes punctuate the coins' falling. We might be tempted to consider the synchronism silly; but we must not forget that these coins are the money of betrayal, the money of Judas. The fall of the four coins is fatal: they open a running account that will culminate in the informer's condemnation. (It is by adding up all Gypo's expenditures and realizing their total equals the amount of the reward for Frankie that the independence fighters confirm their suspicions about Gypo.) All Max Steiner does here is adopt a common technique from opera that uses music for expressive symbolization of actions. Note first that the music does not *substitute* for the sound of the falling coins—the coins are heard diegetically at the same time (more or less). Second, the melodic shape here is precisely that of one of the score's leitmotifs, the betrayal motif.

So what is there about these musical interventions that nevertheless feels like imitation? The answer is that they are punctual and synchronous. As we shall see below (and as I wrote in *La Toile trouée*, in the chapter on "the clapboard"), synchronization is an important factor in film in how it manages to glue together entirely unlikely sounds and images.[5] In opera the frequent synchronizing of music and action poses no problem, since it is an integral part of an overall gestural and decorative stylization. In the cinema such synchronization must be handled more discreetly, so as not to be taken as exclusively imitative or slip over into the mode of cartoon gags. And if *The Informer*'s attempts at operatic stylization have aged ungracefully in using this overt synchronism, we can still recognize the film for its daring and honesty. The cinema is a realist art: but it remains that this realist art has progressed only by means of straining against its own principle, through forceful doses of unrealism.

What makes the use of music unique in certain scenes of *The Informer*, what gives it a quality that might seem tedious? It's the way the music stops. Music cues do not get eclipsed by such things as doors opening or closing, as they would learn to do later in the thirties. Instead, music in *The Informer* often gets interrupted bluntly and suddenly, in mid-phrase, producing a silence in which the subsequent dialogue resonates strangely. By stopping and passing the baton to speech, it seems as if the music is pointedly referring to itself rather than remaining unobtrusive. Henceforth the cinema would tend to avoid this abrupt and conspicuous transition, preferring a more fluid relationship wherein music and scene were mixed more thoroughly together; music became more constant and at the same time more indistinct.

Punctuation: Elements of Auditory Setting

I call *elements of auditory setting* (E.A.S.) sounds with a more or less punctual source, which appear more or less intermittently and which help to create and define a film's space by means of specific, distinct small touches. Typical sounds of the auditory setting are the faraway barking of a dog, or the ringing of a phone in the office next door, or a police car siren. The E.A.S. inhabits and defines a space, unlike a "permanent" sound such as the continuous chirping of birds or the noise of ocean surf that *is* the space itself.

Beyond its narrative role (establishing or reestablishing the framework of the action), the E.A.S. can also have a punctuative role, thanks to editing. It can be used with intelligence to help create the scene's overall rhythm; this possibility can renew and transfigure its functions completely.

The multiplicity of functions of elements of auditory setting reminds us that soundtrack analysis must constantly take into account the likelihood of overdetermination: that is, a filmic element often signifies on several different levels at once.

Anticipation: Convergence/Divergence

From a horizontal perspective sounds and images are not uniform elements all lined up like fenceboards in a row. They have tendencies, they indicate directions, they follow patterns of change and repetition that create in the spectator a sense of hope, expectation, and plenitude to be broken or emptiness to be filled. This effect is best known in connection with music. Musical form leads the listener to expect cadences; the listener's anticipation of the cadence comes to subtend his/her perception. Likewise, a camera movement, a sound rhythm, or a change in an actor's behavior can put the spectator in a state of anticipation. What follows either confirms or surprises the expectations established— and thus an audiovisual sequence functions according to this dynamic of anticipation and outcome.

One of the most persistent players of this game is Godard, in his *Letter to Freddy Buache*. Ravel's *Bolero*, the music he selected to accompany the whole video, is a vast melodic curve that prepares for but ceaselessly defers its cadence, like a delayed orgasm—while for its part Godard's voiceover commentary takes a malicious pleasure in fishing about for the right words, thus making us wait for them—meantime constant pans in the image leave us to imagine, at the end of the paths they trace through urban or bucolic landscapes, who knows what revelation.

In an audiovisual sequence the audio-viewer consciously or unconsciously recognizes the beginnings of a pattern (e.g., a crescendo or an accelerando) and then verifies whether it evolves as expected. It is often more interesting when the expectation is subverted. And, at other times, when everything ensues as anticipated, the sweetness and perfection of the rendering of the anticipation itself are sufficient to move us.

In *Children of a Lesser God*, just after William Hurt has left the dance and walks out into the night air he turns around to see Marlee Matlin, all dressed in white, coming to join him. The volume of the music from the dance gradually decreases, faded out by the mixer. Consciously the spectator expects the two characters to meet; less consciously, for the music to disappear when the lovers join—for there to be silence when they touch. This indeed is what happens, the convergence of a joining and a disappearance, but so precisely and subtly executed that we are always moved when the disco music fades into silence, and the reunited couple become still, all in one breath.

We never stop anticipating, and surprising anticipation—for this is the movement of desire itself.

Separating: Silence

In a well-known aphorism Bresson reminded us that the sound film made silence possible. This statement illuminates a paradox:

it was necessary to have sounds and voices so that the *interruption* of them could probe more deeply into this thing called silence. (In the silent cinema, everything just suggested sounds.)

However, this zero-degree (or is it?) element of the soundtrack that is silence is certainly not so simple to achieve, even on the technical level. You can't just interrupt the auditory flow and stick in a few inches of blank leader. The spectator would have the impression of a technical break (which of course Godard used to full effect, notably in *Band of Outsiders*). Every place has its own unique silence, and it is for this reason that for sound recording on exterior locations, in a studio, or in an auditorium, care is taken to record several seconds of the "silence" specific to that place. This ambient silence can be used later if needed behind dialogue, and will create the desired feeling that the space of the action is temporarily silent.

However, the impression of silence in a film scene does not simply come from an absence of noise. It can only be produced as a result of context and preparation. The simplest of cases consists in preceding it with a noise-filled sequence. So silence is never a neutral emptiness. It is the negative of sound we've heard beforehand or imagined; it is the product of a contrast.

Another way to express silence, which might or might not be associated with the procedures I have just described, consists in subjecting the listener to . . . noises. But I mean here the subtle kind of noises like the ticking of an alarm clock, naturally associated with calmness. These do not attract attention; they are not even audible unless other sounds (of traffic, conversation, the workplace) cease.

We find a good example in *Alien*, when Ridley Scott, with a closeup of the cat who is the space ship's mascot, wants to create the impression of a disconcerting silence to precede sinister developments. The shots leading up to this are sonically rich, preparing for the void that follows, but care has been taken that the silence doesn't strike too suddenly. During the first three seconds of the shot of the cat we can hear a small unidentified sound, like a tick-tock. Its presence on the soundtrack, then its rapid fadeout, help form a bridge to total emptiness.

In *Face to Face* Bergman gets a very different effect by a reverse treatment of the same kind of ticking sound. A woman, deeply depressed, is at home getting ready for bed. The ticking of the alarm clock on the night table, which had previously gone unnoticed, becomes louder and louder. Paradoxically we end up with an anxiety-producing impression of silence, all the stronger because the only sound there is is so intense, and heightened by the lack of other sounds, bringing out this emptiness in a terrible way. (Bergman's personal touch can be noted here in the swift precision with which the sound is augmented.)

Film uses other sounds as synonyms of silence: faraway animal calls, clocks in an adjoining room, rustlings, and all the intimate noises of immediate space. Also, and somewhat strangely, a hint of reverberation added to isolated sounds (for example, footsteps in a street) can reinforce the feeling of emptiness and silence. We cannot perceive reverb like this when other sounds (e.g., daytime traffic) are heard at the same time.

POINT OF SYNCHRONIZATION AND SYNCHRESIS

A *point of synchronization*, or synch point, is a salient moment of an audiovisual sequence during which a sound event and a visual event meet in synchrony. It is a point where the effect of synchresis (see below) is particularly prominent, rather like an accented chord in music.

The phenomenon of significant synch points generally obeys laws of gestalt psychology. A synch point sometimes emerges more specially in a sequence:

· As an unexpected double break in the audiovisual flow, a synchronous cut in both sound and image track. This is characteristic of external logic, frequent in *Alien* for example.

· As a form of punctuation at the end of a sequence whose tracks seemed separate until they end up together (synch point of convergence).

· Purely by its physical character: for example when the synch point falls on a closeup that creates an effect of visual fortissimo, or when the sound itself is louder than the rest of the soundtrack.

· But also by its affective or semantic character: a word of dialogue that conveys a strong meaning and is spoken in a certain way can be the locus of an important point of synchronization with the image.

A point of synchronization can stage the meeting of elements of quite differing natures. For example, a visual cut can be coordinated with a word or group of words specially emphasized by the voiceover commentary. In Godard's *Letter to Freddy Buache* several meetings between visual cuts and ends of sentences provide the principal synch points on which the architecture of the whole film is based. The synch point is indeed the place where the audiovisual "arch" meets the ground before taking off again.

Synch points naturally signify in relation to the content of the scene and the film's overall dynamics. As such, they give the audiovisual flow its phrasing, just as chords or cadences, which are also vertical meetings of elements, can give phrasing to a sequence of music.

There is also the particular case we shall call the *false synch point*. The deceptive or false cadence in Western classical music is a cadence that a particular harmonic progression sets us up for but that does not resolve as anticipated. In much the same way audiovisual texts have false synch points. They can be more striking than synch points that actually do occur, because the audio-spectator has been given them to fabricate mentally. The best-known example is the suicide scene of a corrupt and compromised official in John Huston's *The Asphalt Jungle*. We see him lock himself into his office, open a drawer, take out the gun; then, we hear the gunshot only, because the visual editing transports us elsewhere. For reasons of taste? Not entirely . . .

Godard scatters the seeds of false synch points at the beginning of *Hail Mary*. We hear repeated plops, and in the image we see only the surface of a lake rippled by something fallen into it; the fallen object, and the place of the fall, remain offscreen. So the cause is heard on the soundtrack while its consequences shimmer in the image. But in the spectator's mind is a synch point all the more disturbing for being postulated but not actualized (into hearing and seeing what falls); the object in question, acousmatic, may be anything one wishes: a stone someone has tossed, a meteorite, or the Holy Spirit.

Emblematic Synch Point: The Punch

In real life a punch does not necessarily make noise, even if it hurts someone. In a cinematic or televisual audio-image, the sound of the impact is well-nigh obligatory. Otherwise no one would believe the punches, even if they had really been inflicted. Accordingly they are accompanied with sound effects as a matter of course. This punctual, momentary, abrupt coincidence of a sound and a visible impact thus becomes the most direct and immediate representation of the audiovisual synch point, in its quality as the sequence's keystone, punctuation, Lacan's *point de capiton*. The punch becomes the moment around which the narration's time is constructed: beforehand, it is thought about, it is announced, it is dreaded; afterward, we feel its shock waves, we confront its reverberations. It is the audiovisual point toward which everything converges and out from which all radiates. And it is also the privileged expression of instantaneity in the audio-image.

The ultrabrief image of the punch all by itself would not become engraved into the memory, would tend to get lost. But an ultrabrief but clearly delineated *sound* has the advantage of etching its form and tone directly into consciousness, where it can repeat as an echo. Sound is the rubber stamp that marks the image with the seal of instantaneity. (On the metaphor of the stamp recall the gag of the librarian in Spielberg's *Indiana Jones and the Last Crusade*.)

What is the most important object in audiovisual representation? The human body. What can the most immediate and brief meeting between two of these objects be? The physical blow. And what is the most immediate audiovisual relationship? The synchronization between a blow heard and a blow seen—or one that we believe we have seen. For, in fact, we do not really see the punch; you can confirm this by cutting the sound out of a scene. What we hear is what we haven't had time to see.

Accented Synch Points and Temporal Elasticity

This structure is already present in much nonanimation cinema, notably in all martial arts and fight films. But Japanese animated films I can see on French television add something more: an analysis of movement (as in Muybridge and Marey's famous photos, which lie at cinema's origins), the use of slow motion and radical stylization of time. These diverse techniques get their inspiration from the slow-motion and still-frames of sports replays, but also directly from Japanese comic books, or *mangas*. In these rudimentary animated adventures the point of synchronization constituted by the punch, this point of hooking auditory continuity to visual continuity, is what allows the time around it to swell, fold, puff up, tighten, stretch or, on the contrary, to gape or hang loosely like fabric. On either side of a characteristic synch point such as a punch the capacity for temporal elasticity can become almost infinite. During an episode of the series *Dragon Ball* the battling characters constantly freeze in mid-motion, stop in mid-air (for they make incredible leaps), and converse interminably, slowing down, speeding up and changing poses like a series of discontinuous slides, before launching flurries of swift punches and kicks to one another.

In short, the punch with sound effects is to audiovisual language as the chord is to music, mobilizing the vertical dimension. In the brutal and exhausting boxing scenes in *Raging Bull* Scorsese used punches to bestow a maximum degree of temporal elasticity on the fighting scenes; thus he could use slow motion, repeated images, and so forth.

The paradox is that in the beginning, temporal elasticity was an inherent characteristic of the silent cinema. Since the silents did not have to be dubbed point by point and second by second with synchronous sound, they could easily dilate and contract time. With the arrival of sound this elasticity began to disappear from the sound film. And though it may have succeeded in entering into a few realist films, note that it shows up most insistently in action and combat sequences, such as Sam Peckinpah's. In other words, temporal flexibility was not introduced into a sound-image relationship that is vague and asynchronous but, on the contrary, it appears in scenes that have strong points of synchronization, where blows, collisions, and explosions can serve as strong reference points.

Synchresis

Synchresis (a word I have forged by combining *synchronism* and *synthesis*) is the spontaneous and irresistible weld produced between a particular auditory phenomenon and visual phenomenon when they occur at the same time. This join results independently of any rational logic. Synchresis is responsible for our conviction that the sounds heard over the shots of the hands in the prologue of *Persona* are indeed the sounds of the hammer pounding nails into them.

Synchresis is what makes dubbing, postsynchronization, and sound-effects mixing possible, and enables such a wide array of choice in these processes. For a single body and a single face on the screen, thanks to synchresis, there are dozens of allowable voices—just as, for a shot of a hammer, any one of a hundred sounds will do.

Certain experimental videos and films demonstrate that synchresis can even work out of thin air—that is, with images and sounds that strictly speaking have nothing to do with each other, forming monstrous yet inevitable and irresistible agglomerations in our perception. The syllable *fa* is heard over a shot of a dog, the sound of a blow with the sight of a triangle. Synchresis is Pavlovian.

But it is not totally automatic. It is also a function of meaning, and is organized according to gestaltist laws and contextual determinations. Play a stream of random audio and visual events, and you will find that certain ones will come together through synchresis and other combinations will not. The sequence takes on its phrasing all on its own, getting caught up in patterns of mutual reinforcement and phenomena of "good form" that do not operate by any simple rules. Sometimes this logic is obvious. When there is a sound that is louder than the others, it coagulates with the image it is heard with more strongly than previous or subsequent images and sounds. Meaning and rhythm can also play important roles in securing the synchresis effect.

For some situations that set up precise expectations of sound—a character walking, for example—synchresis is unstoppable, and we can therefore use just about any sound effects for these footsteps that we might desire. In *Mon Oncle* Tati drew on all kinds of noises for human footsteps, including ping-pong balls and glass objects.

The effect of synchresis is obviously capable of being influenced, reinforced, and oriented by cultural habits. But at the same time it very probably has an innate basis, as shown by the limit experiments of video artist Gary Hill.[6] Specific reactions to synchronized aural and visual phenomena have been observed in newborn infants.

The "modest" phenomenon of synchresis—modest because it is so common—opens the floodgates of sound film. Synchresis permits filmmakers to make the most subtle and astonishing audiovisual configurations. But today, when it has become commonplace to see a moving figure on a screen as we hear movement, it is difficult to imagine the amazement inspired by the first synchronized sound films in the twenties. That sound and image were heard and seen like a couple of perfectly matched dancers was a spectacle in itself. Texts written at the time bear witness to this state of mind. So do the films, especially the musical ones, which exalted synchronism as such, showing violinists or banjo players whose every visual gesture provoked a distinct sound on the soundtrack.

Habit has led us to consider this phenomenon "natural" and devoid of cinematic interest. But let us rediscover it.

Loose and Tight Synchronisms

Synchresis does not function in an all-or-nothing way. There are degrees of synchronism and, particularly in the case of lip synch, these "degrees" play a part in determining film style. For example, the French, who are accustomed to a tight and narrow synchronization, find fault with the postsynching of Italian films. What they are objecting to in reality is a looser and more "forgiving" synchronization that's often off by a tenth of a second or so. This difference is particularly noticeable in the case of the voice. While very tight synch holds voices to lip movements, Italian films synch more loosely, taking into consideration the totality of the speaking body, particularly gestures.

In general, loose synch gives a less naturalistic, more readily poetic effect, and a very tight synch stretches the audiovisual canvas more . . . this canvas, the status of whose landscape or "scene" we now shall proceed to investigate.

FOUR

THE AUDIOVISUAL

SCENE

.   .   .

IS THERE AN AUDITORY SCENE?

"The Image" = The Frame

Why in the cinema do we speak of "the image" in the singular, when a film has thousands of them (only several hundred if it's shots we're counting, but these too are ceaselessly changing)? The reason is that even if there were millions, there would still be only one container for them, the frame. What "the image" designates in the cinema is not content but container: the frame.

The frame can start out black and empty for a few seconds (Ophuls's *Le Plaisir*, Preminger's *Laura*) or even for several minutes (Duras's *L'Homme Atlantique*). But it nevertheless remains perceivable and present for the spectator as the visible, rectangular, delimited place of the projection. The frame thus affirms itself as a preexisting container, which was there before the images came on and which can remain after the images disappear (end credits reaffirm this role in a certain way).[1]

What is specific to film is that it has just *one place for images*—as opposed to video installations, slide shows, Sound and Light shows, and other multimedia genres, which can have several. This fact, and no other, accounts for why we speak of the image in the singular.

Let us recall that in the first years of the cinematograph people sought to soften the hard borders of the frame, through irising, masking, or haloing, similar to such effects in photography. But these techniques were abandoned little by little, and, aside from the rare experiment with changing frame dimensions within a single film (Max Ophuls in *Lola Montès*), the principle of the full-frame image came to dominate in 99 percent of movies. Similarly, the occasional experiment with multiscreen cinema—Abel Gance's *Napoleon*, Michael Wadleigh's *Woodstock*, or even Paul Morissey's *Forty Deuce*—have not spawned many descendants, and as exceptions they prove the rule of the classical frame.

There Is No Auditory Container for Sounds

What is the corresponding case for sound? The exact opposite. For sound there is neither frame nor preexisting container. We can pile up as many sounds on the soundtrack as we wish without reaching a limit. Further, these sounds can be situated at different narrative levels, such as conventional background music (nondiegetic) and synch dialogue (diegetic)—while visual elements can hardly ever be located at more than one of these levels at once. So there is no auditory container for film sounds, nothing analogous to this visual container of the images that is the frame.

What do sounds do when put together with a film image? They dispose themselves in relation to the frame and its content. Some are embraced as synchronous and onscreen, others wander at the surface and on the edges as offscreen. And still others position themselves clearly outside the diegesis, in an imaginary orchestra pit (nondiegetic music), or on a sort of balcony, the place of voiceovers. In short, we classify sounds in relation to what we see in the image, and this classification is constantly subject to revision, depending on changes in what we see. Thus we can define most cinema as "a place of images, plus sounds," with sound being "that which seeks its place."[2] This relation differs from that of television, as we will see later on.

If we can speak of an audiovisual scene, it is because the scenic space has boundaries, it is structured by the edges of the visual frame. Film sound is that which is contained or not contained *in an image*; there is no place of the sounds, no auditory scene already preexisting in the soundtrack—and therefore, properly speaking, *there is no soundtrack*.

But Jean-Marie Straub's and Danièle Huillet's highly idiosyncratic 1969 film *Othon* (which acts out a Roman tragedy by Corneille on modern-day Roman locations) demonstrates what a sound scene or an auditory container-of-sounds might be in a monaural film. We'd have to agree that the sounds are the actors' voices declaiming their lines, and that the container would be the urban hum of distant traffic in which the voices and lines are heard. Actors in *Othon* often give long monologues offscreen, and yet such voices are not perceived as the traditional offscreen voice entirely determined by the image. Their voices seem to be "in the same place" as voices of actors we do see, a space defined by the background noise. A related effect can be felt in another film of the same year, Jacques Rivette's *La Religieuse*. Here, the reverb around voices, which results from direct sound (as with Straub and Huillet), has a similar role of enveloping and homogenizing the voices, inscribing them in a space like the medium of city traffic noise does in *Othon*. The price each film pays is a relative loss of intelligibility. Generally speaking, certain effects of the "spatial signature," as Rick Altman calls it, can provide the framework for an auditory scene.[3]

At least all this holds true until the arrival of Dolby, which now creates a space with fluid borders, a sort of superscreen enveloping the screen—the superfield, which I expand upon in a later chapter. But the superfield does not altogether upset the structure we have described, even if it has set it trembling on its base.

How the Image "Magnetizes" Sound in Space

What does a sound typically lead us to ask about space? Not "Where is it?"—for the sound "is" in the air we breathe or, if you will, as a perception it's in our head—but rather, "Where does it come from?" The problem of localizing a sound therefore most often translates as the problem of locating its source.

Traditional monaural film presents a strange sensory experience in this regard. The point from which sounds physically issue is often not the same as the point on the screen where these sounds are supposed to be coming from, but the spectator nevertheless does perceive the sounds as coming from these "sources" on the screen. In the case of footsteps, for example, if the character is walking across the screen, the sound of the footsteps seems to follow his image, even though in the real space of the movie theater, they continue to issue from the same stationary loudspeaker. If the character is offscreen, we perceive the footsteps as if they are outside the field of vision—an "outside" that's more mental than physical.

Moreover, if under particular screening conditions the loud-speaker is not located behind the screen, but placed somewhere else in the auditorium or in an outdoor setting (e.g., at the drive-in), or if the soundtrack resonates in our head by means of ear-phones (watching a movie on an airplane), these sounds will be perceived no less as coming from the screen, in spite of the evidence of our own senses.

This means that in the cinema there is *spatial magnetization* of sound by image. When we perceive a sound as being offscreen or located at screen right this is a psychological phenomenon, at least if a monaural projection is involved.

During the first years of multitrack sound, attempts at real spatialization were made—that is, really locating the sound on the left side of the screen if its source was shown there. The problem with these efforts is precisely that they ran into this psychological phenomenon of spatialization. Mental spatialization had been a blessing for the sound film, since it allowed movies to function for well over forty years without problems. We only need imagine the mess if sounds had to issue from the points where their sources on the screen were shown: one would have to install veritable beehives of speakers behind and around the screen. Not to mention, of course, the headaches of sound matching that would have resulted.

In using Dolby today filmmakers have learned the lesson from these first efforts in realistic spatialization and their "in-the-wing effects" (see p. 83). Today's multitrack mixes very often strike a compromise between psychological localization and real localization.

Note that sound coming from another point than the screen is "magnetizable" only if the sound itself maintains a basic spatial stability. If it constantly moves back and forth among loudspeakers, the image will have a harder time absorbing it, and the sound takes on a centrifugal force of its own that resists visual "attraction."

Even in the classic case of a single loudspeaker, there is one real sonic dimension that the sound cinema capitalized on in its infancy, and neglected later: depth, the sensation of distance from the source. The ear detects depth from such indices as a reduced harmonic spectrum, softened attacks and transitions, a different blend of direct sound and reflected sound, and the presence of reverberation. The factor of depth has figured importantly in experiments with sound perspective in some films.[4] Let us note, however, that sound perspective was not so much a true depth, necessarily situating the sound source to the rear of the spatial plane of the screen, as a *distance* interpreted by the spectator in various different directions, depending on what she or he saw on the screen and could infer about the place of the source. In other words, a distant sound can be interpreted as being distantly to the left, far to the right, far behind the spectator, far to the rear of the screen; in other words, always localized in space depending on mental factors.

Thus to mental localization, determined more by what we see than by what we hear (or rather by the relationship between the two), we may oppose the absolute spatialization made possible by multitrack film sound.

THE ACOUSMATIC

Acousmatic, a word of Greek origin discovered by Jérôme Peignot and theorized by Pierre Schaeffer, describes "sounds one hears without seeing their originating cause."[5] Radio, phonograph, and telephone, all which transmit sounds without showing their emitter, are acousmatic media by definition. The term *acousmatic music* has also been coined; composer Francis Bayle, for example, uses it to designate concert music that is made for a recorded medium, intentionally eliminating the possibility of seeing the sounds' initial causes.

What can we call the opposite of acousmatic sound? Schaeffer proposed "direct," but since this word lends itself to so much ambiguity, we shall coin the term *visualized* sound—i.e., accompanied by the sight of its source or cause.

In a film an acousmatic situation can develop along two different scenarios: either a sound is visualized first, and subsequently acousmatized, or it is acousmatic to start with, and is visualized only afterward. The first case associates a sound with a precise image from the outset. This image can then reappear with greater or lesser distinctness in the spectator's mind each time the sound is heard acousmatically. It will be an "embodied" sound, identified with an image, demythologized, classified.[6]

The second case, common to moody mystery films, keeps the sound's cause a secret, before revealing all. The acousmatic sound maintains suspense, constituting a dramatic technique in itself. A theatrical analogy to this treatment of sound might be to announce and then to delay a stage entrance; think of Tartuffe, who finally enters during the third act of Molière's play. The cinema gives us the famous example of *M*; for as long as possible the film conceals the physical appearance of the child-murderer, even though we hear his voice and his maniacal whistling from the very beginning. Lang preserves the mystery of the character as long as he can, before "de-acousmatizing" him.[7]

A sound or voice that remains acousmatic creates a mystery of the nature of its source, its properties and its powers, given that causal listening cannot supply complete information about the sound's nature and the events taking place.

It's fairly common in films to see evil, awe-inspiring, or otherwise powerful characters introduced through sound before they are subsequently thrown out to the pasture of visibility, de-acousmatized. Odile Larère has discussed the example of Visconti's *Conversation Piece*, where the intruders who disturb the lovely universe of the hero, the old professor played by Burt Lancaster, systematically make their entrance on the soundtrack before being visible.[8]

The opposition between visualized and acousmatic provides a basis for the fundamental audiovisual notion of offscreen space.

THE QUESTION OF OFFSCREEN SPACE

Onscreen, Offscreen, Nondiegetic

The question of offscreen sound has long dominated an entire field of thinking and theorizing about film sound, and it occupies a central place in my first two books on sound as well. Although we can see now that it seems to have been privileged at the expense of other avenues of investigation, it has yet to lose its importance as a central problem—even if the recent evolution of film sound, involving mainly multitrack sound and the "super-field" it establishes, has modified some of its basic traits.

In the narrow sense *offscreen sound* in film is sound that is acousmatic, relative to what is shown in the shot: sound whose source is invisible, whether temporarily or not. We call *onscreen sound* that whose source appears in the image, and belongs to the reality represented therein.

Third, to designate sound whose supposed source is not only absent from the image but is also external to the story world, I shall use the term *nondiegetic*.[9] This is the widespread case of voiceover commentary and narration and, of course, musical underscoring.

Do Exceptions Disprove the Rule?

In *Le Son au cinéma* I presented onscreen, offscreen, and nondiegetic as three zones of a circle, wherein each communicates with the other two:

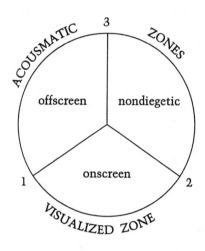

1. Onscreen/offscreen border
2. Onscreen/nondiegetic border
3. Offscreen/nondiegetic border

But in recent years, the distinction onscreen-offscreen-non-diegetic, which arises from very basic considerations, has often been denounced as obsolete and reductive. Critics have problematized it with increasing fervor, because of the exceptions and special cases it doesn't seem to account for. For example, where should we situate sounds (usually voices) that come from electrical devices located in the action and that the image suggests or directly shows: telephone receivers, radios, public-address speakers? And what to do with a character who speaks with her back to us, so we don't actually see her speak? Is her voice acousmatic (offscreen)? And what can we say about the so-called internal voice of a character who can be seen in the image—the voices of his conscience, of his memory, of his imaginings and fantasies?[10]

What about Amy Heckerling's *Look Who's Talking*, where an adult voice accompanies the facial expressions of a baby, and articulates the baby's thoughts and feelings when the baby obviously doesn't have the physical and intellectual ability to do so? The voice is definitely connected to the present of the action, but it is not visualizable; so it seems unconcerned with these distinctions, being tied to the image via the loosest of synchronization. And finally how should we classify general background sounds such as birdsongs and wind, heard with natural exteriors? It seems rather ridiculous to characterize them as offscreen, on the basis that we don't "see" the little birds chirping or the wind blowing.

These exceptions, though distressing, do not by any means cancel out the validity or interest of a basic distinction between onscreen, offscreen, and nondiegetic sound, or of the basic division between acousmatic and visualized.

A Topological and Spatial Perspective

Anyone who brings up such exceptions in order to claim the categories useless or trivial is throwing out the baby with the bathwater. Why reject a valuable distinction simply because it isn't absolute? It is a mistake to see things in a binary, all-or-nothing logic. These distinctions only have meaning from a geographical, topological, and spatial perspective, analogous to zones among which one finds many shadings, degrees, and ambiguities. Of course we must continue to refine and fill in our typology of film sound. We must add new categories—not claiming thereby to exhaust all possibilities, but at least to enlarge the scope, to recognize, define, and develop new areas.

Ambient Sound (Territory-Sound)

Let us call *ambient sound* sound that envelops a scene and inhabits its space, without raising the question of the identification or visual embodiment of its source: birds singing, churchbells ringing. We might also call them *territory sounds*, because they serve to identify a particular locale through their pervasive and continuous presence.

Internal Sound

Internal sound is sound which, although situated in the present action, corresponds to the physical and mental interior of a character. These include physiological sounds of breathing, moans or heartbeats, all of which could be named *objective-internal* sounds. Also in this category of internal sounds are mental voices, memories, and so on, which I call *subjective-internal* sounds.

Bruce Willis's voice in *Look Who's Talking* gives us an interesting case of an internal voice, partly externalized through gesture. The film establishes it as not being heard by the other characters. In the voice of the adult that the baby will become, it tells us what the baby might be thinking, even as this voice is associated with the gestures in a way that is faithful to codes of realism regarding the baby's physical abilities.

"On-the-Air" Sound

I shall refer to sounds in a scene that are supposedly transmitted electronically as *on-the-air*—transmitted by radio, telephone, amplification, and so on—sounds that consequently are not subject to "natural" mechanical laws of sound propagation. In fact, to an ever greater degree, these sounds from television sets, clock radios, and intercoms are taking on a unique status in the films they appear in. Sometimes we hear them in sound closeup—clear and sharp, as if the film's loudspeaker were directly plugged into the radio, telephone, or phonograph depicted on the screen. At the other extreme thay can be identified in the setting by acoustical traits to produce an effect of distancing, reverb, and the particular tone color of the speakers or whatever their onscreen source is. Between these two cases lie infinite degrees of variation. On-the-air sounds, usually situated in the scene's real time, enjoy the freedom of crossing boundaries of cinematic space.

A particular case of on-the-air sound is that of recorded or broadcast music. Depending on the particular weight given by such factors as mixing, levels, use of filters, and conditions of music recording—i.e., whether the emphasis is on the sound's *initial source* (the real instruments that play, the voice that sings) or on the *terminal source* (the speaker present in the narrative whose material presence is felt through use of filters, static, and reverb), the sound of on-the-air music can transcend or blur the zones of onscreen, offscreen, and nondiegetic. It can also be read, to greater or lesser degrees, as screen music or pit music. Road movies such as Barry Levinson's *Rain Man* constantly play with this oscillation. As early as 1975 George Lucas's *American Graffiti*—with the help of its sound designer Walter Murch—explored the entire gamut of possibilities between these two poles. The film was based on the simple setup of placing its characters in their cars for much of the action, all listening to a single rock-and-roll station.

The same problem exists for *dialogue* presented in the diegesis as recorded: does it refer to the time of its production or to the time at which we are hearing it? Imagine a scene in a film where a man is listening to a taped interview. If the sound being listened to has technical qualities of directness and presence, it refers back to the circumstances of its original state. If it has aural qualities that highlight its "recordedness," and if there is emphasis on the acoustic properties of the place where it is being listened to in the diegesis, we tend to focus on the moment where the recording is being heard. In *The Passenger* there is a sequence where Jack Nicholson listens to the recording of a conversation he had with a man he met by chance. Antonioni shuttles from one position to the other and in this way leads into a flashback. The interview Nicholson is listening to becomes real, becomes the scene of the interview itself.

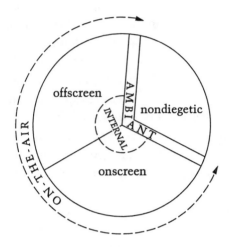

So our tripartite circle becomes more complicated, but also richer. Through the very exceptions we introduce, it continues to illustrate the dimensions and oppositions involved:

· the opposition between acousmatic and visualized,
· the opposition between objective and subjective or real and imagined,
· the differences between past, present, and future.

It is important to think of the circle as consisting of interlocking sectors. In fact, this would probably be expressed much better by a topological model in three dimensions. We also return to the question of the *source*, which conditions such distinctions. First, the idea of sound source must be relativized and "unpacked," since "the" sound source is usually a multifaceted phenomenon. And second, the making and even the conception of a film and its screenplay are likely to emphasize one of these facets to a greater or lesser degree.

Place of the Sound, Place of the Source

Spatially speaking, a sound and its source are two different entities. In a film the emphasis may fall on one or the other, and the onscreen-offscreen question will pose itself differently, according to which thing—the sound or its cause—the spectator reads as being "in" the image or "outside" it. For sound and cause, though quite distinct, are almost always confused. But surely this confusion is inscribed also at the very heart of our experience itself, like an unsettling knot of problems.

For example, the sound of a shoe's heel striking the floor of a reverberant room has a very particular source. But as sound, as an agglomerate of many reflections on different surfaces, it can fill as big a volume as the room in which it resonates. In fact, no matter how precisely a sound's source can be identified, the sound in itself is by definition a phenomenon that tends to spread out, like a gas, into whatever available space there is.

In the case of ambient sounds, which are often the product of multiple specific and local sources (a brook, bird songs), what is important is the space inhabited and defined by the sound, more than its multisource origin. The same goes for films of musical performances. Depending on choices in the editing and technical directing of sound and image, the emphasis can fall either on the specific material source of the sound (the instrument, the singer) or on the sound as it fills the auditory space, considered independently from the source.

The more reverberant the sound, the more it tends to express the space that contains it. The deader it is, the more it tends to refer to its material source. The voice represents a special case. In a film, when the voice is heard in sound closeup without reverb, it is likely to be at once the voice the spectator internalizes as his or her own and the voice that takes total possession of the diegetic space. It is both completely internal and invading the entire universe. This is what I have called the *I-Voice*.[11] Of course the voice owes this special status to the fact that it is the original, definitive sound that both fills us and comes from us.

In the play of onscreen and offscreen space, background music also stands out as a type of exception that proves the overall rule.

The Exception of Music

I have given the name *pit music* to music that accompanies the image from a nondiegetic position, outside the space and time of the action. The term refers to the classical opera's orchestra pit. I shall refer as *screen music*, on the other hand, to music arising from a source located directly or indirectly in the space and time of the action, even if this source is a radio or an offscreen musician.

These ideas were developed in chapters on music in *Le Son au cinéma*. They correspond to a distinction that has long been noted, with a variety of names. Some say nondiegetic for the first and diegetic for the second, or commentative and actual, or objective and subjective. For music I prefer to rely on terms that simply designate the place where each (supposedly) comes from. A music cue inscribed in the action can of course be just as "commentative" as a nondiegetic music cue, as in Siodmak's *Abschied*, where the protagonists' neighbor is a pianist whose music accompanies and punctuates their emotional states. *Rear Window* conclusively demonstrates this as well.

Once this distinction is established it is relatively simple to describe ambiguous or mixed cases. Consider the case of screen music framed by a pit music cue with ampler orchestration: someone plays a piano in the action, to the accompaniment of the pit orchestra. This occurs in many musicals; an example that comes to mind is in Raoul Walsh's *The King and Four Queens*. In another kind of case music begins as screen music and continues as pit music by separating from the action. Or, inversely, a grand pit music cue can narrow into screen music being played by an instrument onscreen, for example in older movies, when opening credit music segues into the start of the action.

Not to mention the numerous cases in current films where music established as on-the-air freely circulates between the two levels. In *Taxi Driver* Bernard Herrmann's main theme, heard as pit music throughout much of the film, crops up as the music on a phonograph to which the pimp (Harvey Keitel) and his young hooker (Jodie Foster) dance.

Music as Spatiotemporal Turntable

All music in a film, especially pit music, can function like the spatiotemporal equivalent of a railroad switch. This is to say that music enjoys the status of being a little freer of barriers of time and space than the other sound and visual elements. The latter are obliged to remain clearly defined in their relation to the diegetic space and to a linear and chronological notion of time.

Another way to put it is that music is cinema's *passe-muraille*, capable of instantly communicating with the other elements of the action.[12] For example, it can accompany from the nondiegetic realm a character who is onscreen. Music can swing over from pit to screen at a moment's notice, without in the least throwing into question the integrity of the diegesis, as a voiceover intervening in the action would. No other auditory element can claim this privilege. Out of time and out of space, music communicates with all times and all spaces of a film, even as it leaves them to their separate and distinct existences.

Music can aid characters in crossing great distances and long stretches of time almost instantaneously. This use of music is fairly frequent, ever since the beginning of sound. In King Vidor's *Hallelujah* protagonist Zeke moves through several locales during the singing of one spiritual, "Going Home": a boat on the Mississippi, the roof of a train, a prairie. We can recognize here the embryonic structure of the music video, which, governed by musical form (its only constraint being to include points of synchronization here and there to solder the music and image together) allows the image to wander at will through time and space. In the music video there really no longer exists an audiovisual scene anchored in coherent time and space.

In Vidor's film music gives the characters winged feet; it functions to contract both space and time. In general, however, we can say that music makes space and time pliable, subject to contraction *or* distention. In suspense scenes, it is music that makes us accept the convention of a frozen moment, eternalized by editing.

And in the long confrontations in Sergio Leone's films, where characters do little but pose like statues staring at each other, Ennio Morricone's music is crucial in creating the sense of temporal immobilization. True, Leone also tried to stretch time without the help of music. Notably, at the opening of *Once Upon a Time in the West*, he made do with the occasional creaking of a weather vane or a noria. But there, the plot situation—a long period of waiting and inaction—was chosen to justify the immobility of the characters. At any rate, Leone developed this sort of epic immobility with reference to opera and by generally using music overtly on the soundtrack.

RELATIVE OFFSCREEN SPACE AND ABSOLUTE OFFSCREEN SPACE

The term *offscreen sound* is deceptive; it might lead us to think that the sound itself has some intrinsic quality. We only have to close our eyes at a film or look away from the screen to register the obvious: without vision, offscreen sounds are just as present—at least as well-defined acoustically speaking—as onscreen sounds. Nothing allows us to tell the two apart. Acousmatized and reduced to an ensemble of sounds that certainly constitute a soundtrack worthy of the name, the film completely changes. I already cited the example of certain scenes of *Mr Hulot's Holiday*: listen to the sounds without the image and they reveal a different character.

Thus sound's "offscreenness," in monaural cinema, is entirely a product of the combination of the visual and aural. It is really a *relation* of what one hears to what one sees, and exists only in this relation; consequently it requires the simultaneous presence of both elements.

Without the image, the sound of numerous great films of the past is meaningless. In particular, the magical voices that fascinated us would atrophy or become prosaic. The voices of Norman's mother in *Psycho*, Dr. Mabuse in *The Testament of Dr. Mabuse*, or Marguerite Duras in *L'Homme Atlantique* would no longer be extraordinary if they ceased to interact with a screen where they encountered the void of their presence.

Multitrack Cinema's "In-the-Wings Effect" and "Offscreen Trash"

Characteristic of real spatialization and of early multitrack sound film experiments, and generally avoided since then, the "in-the-wings effect" is produced whenever a sound linked to a cause likely to appear onscreen, or which has just exited, lingers in one of the offscreen loudspeakers to one side. Examples are the footsteps of a character approaching or leaving, the engine of a car that has just gone offscreen or that is about to appear, or the voice of a protagonist just out of view.

At these times we have the feeling, which is disconcerting to our normal sense of spectatorship, that we're being encouraged to believe that the audiovisual space is literally being extended into the theater beyond the borders of the screen, and that, over the exit sign or above the door to the restrooms, the characters or cars are *there*, preparing their entrance or completing their exit.

Sometimes this in-the-wings effect cannot be attributed to the direction and mixing of the film, but is simply created by an aberrant placement of speakers in the theater. Sometimes it is indeed due to an attempt by the sound engineers or the director to exploit the effect of *absolute offscreen space*, an effect made possible by multitrack.

Slowly, this practice has been dropped. Sounds of entrances and exits are now rendered with greater discretion and subtlety, or they are opportunely drowned in the sound mix (numerous ambient sounds, music) so as to avoid the sense of the nearby offstage wings.

Certainly, the in-the-wings effect created a nagging problem by violating the conventions of continuity editing and making sound matching problematic. But maybe it could have gained more permanent admittance into film practice had it been systematized along with some partial adjustments in editing conventions—just as the superfield of the multitrack cinema was able to strike a compromise with traditional editing. So perhaps it was a mistake to have given it up so quickly.

The *offscreen trash* is a particular case of passive offscreen space (see below) that results from multitrack sound. It is created when the loudspeakers outside the visual field "collect" noises—whistles, thuds, explosions, crashes—which are the product of a catastrophe or a fall at the center of the image. Action and stunt movies often draw on this effect. Sometimes poetic, sometimes intentionally comic, the "offscreen trash" momentarily gives an almost physical existence to objects at the very moment they are dying. A modern action movie like John McTiernan's *Die Hard*, a veritable feast of glass-breaking and deflagration taking place in a tower where a man fights terrorists, is filled with such effects.

Active and Passive Offscreen Sound

I shall give the name *active offscreen sound* to acousmatic sound that raises questions—What is this? What is happening?—whose answer lies offscreen and which incite the look to go there and find out. Such sound creates a curiosity that propels the film forward, and it engages the spectator's anticipation: "I'd like to see his face when the other character says that to him." The sounds in active offscreen space necessarily issue from objects that could be identified by sight. Active offscreen sound is used frequently in traditional sound-image editing, bringing objects and characters into a scene by means of sound, then showing them. Films like *Psycho* are based entirely on the curiosity aroused by active offscreen sound: this mother we keep hearing, what does she look like?

Passive offscreen sound, on the other hand, is sound which creates an atmosphere that envelops and stabilizes the image, without in any way inspiring us to look elsewhere or to anticipate seeing its source. Passive offscreen space does not contribute to the dynamics of editing and scene construction—rather the opposite, since it provides the ear a *stable place* (the general mix of a city's sounds), which permits the editing to move around even more freely in space, to include more close shots, and so on, without disorienting the spectator in space. The principal sounds in passive offscreen space are *territory sounds* and *elements of auditory setting*.

Dolby multitrack has naturally favored the development of passive offscreen space over active. Why? The answer may lie in the fact that active offscreen space mobilizes identifiable, single sources—a human body, an object—and in multitrack sound, real (no longer mental) localization of offscreen sound poses the problem of the too realistic "in-the-wings" effect I have already mentioned. If you want to avoid this effect, it is hardly advisable to employ insistent offscreen sounds that pose enigmas and demand to be de-acousmatized, for, logically speaking, this sound should be situated outside the field of the screen. The entrance of Roy Batty, the antagonist in *Blade Runner*, would have been done by the sound of his voice or his footsteps if the film had been recorded in mono. In the actual film this character is almost always present in the image at the same time as his voice. It is as if we were in a perpetual present. In the traditional monaural cinema, on the other hand, offscreen sound demands its resolution from the center of the image, from the very heart of the image, and thus can be called active.

But as early as 1954 *Rear Window* included much passive offscreen sound: city noise, apartment courtyard sounds, and radio, which, full of reverb, cued the ear into the contextual setting of the scene without raising questions or calling for the visualization of their sources.[13]

EXTENSION

Recall the fixed images, like photographs, in Bergman's *Persona*: shots of the park, a hospital wall, and a pile of dirty snow. Over these shots we heard churchbells and no human sound; these created the impression of a small slumbering village.

Let us take away Bergman's sounds and replace them with, say, the sound of the ocean. We see the same pile of snow, the same grillwork, but offscreen space takes on a salty sea smell. If we now remove the ocean sound and instead dub in a crowd of voices and footsteps, the offscreen space becomes a busy street. Nothing prevents us from taking these same images and beginning with a nearby sound (e.g., footsteps in the snow), then bringing in other sounds that suggest a larger space—car sirens—and so on: someone walks by, the siren passes and fades into the distance, faraway churchbells begin to ring. On one static long take we can thus infinitely dilate the offscreen space imagined and evoked by the soundtrack. And we can shrink it just as easily, in which case we will retain the memory of the vast space evoked at the beginning.

Extension of the the sound environment is our designation for the degree of openness and breadth of the concrete space suggested by sounds, beyond the borders of the visual field, and also within the visual field around the characters.

We can speak of *null extension* when the sonic universe has shrunk to the sounds heard by one single character, possibly including any inner voices he or she hears. At the other end of the spectrum we might call *vast extension* the arrangement wherein, for example, for a scene taking place in a room, we not only hear the sounds in the room (including those offscreen) but also sounds out in the hallway, traffic in the street nearby, a siren farther away, and so on. Ambient extension has no absolute limit except those of the universe—if, of course, sounds could ever be found that were capable of maximally dilating the perception of space surrounding the action.

Obviously what is interesting in the cinema is not only the extension that remains the same throughout a scene and even throughout a film but also contrasts and variations in extension from one scene to another, or even within one and the same scene. Sound designer Walter Murch alludes to variation in extension (without using this term) in describing his work on Coppola's *The Conversation* and *Apocalypse Now*.[14]

Dolby stereo, having dramatically increased the possibilities of layering sounds and deploying them in wide concentric spaces, encourages experimentation with extension. Almost forty years ago *Rear Window*—where everything is seen from a flat in a Greenwich Village courtyard apartment house—made magnificent use of variations in extension. Sometimes it lets us hear the big city thrumming outside this courtyard that the film never leaves. At other times the soundtrack eliminates the larger cityscape entirely, so as to reconcentrate the spectator on the apartment itself, which then becomes for our couple, Grace Kelly and James Stewart, a theater stage cut off from its surroundings. At the very end of the film, the extension becomes extremely narrow, focussing on a single point, like a lone spotlight pursuing a character on a stage—the footsteps of the killer in the stairway, which Stewart can hear approaching . . .

The final scene of *Children of a Lesser God* achieves a similar tightening of spatial extension. As the two estranged lovers reunite in the cool night air, we perceive more and more faintly the noise of a disco dance going on nearby; then it fades down entirely.

Although variations in extension can also consist of sudden contrasts between one scene and the next, they are generally executed in such a way as not to be noticed as a technical manipulation. The occasions on which they *are* made obvious usually contribute toward some emotional effect. This is not like reframings, for example, which are tolerated as technical and coded.

Some films adopt a single fixed strategy for spatial extension and maintain it throughout. In Lang's *M* extension is generally quite limited. All we hear during a conversation scene is what the characters onscreen are saying; almost never do we hear ambient sounds outside the frame. On the other hand, certain modern films adopt a consistently vast extension: think for example of *Blade Runner*, where rumblings of the city behind characters in the frame constantly remind the viewer of the presence of a huge spatial context.

In fact one of the trickiest things in Dolby stereo films is narrowing extension down to one sound or one point in space, since this necessitates silencing several loudspeakers. The final effect of *Rear Window*, for example, would be very difficult in multitrack sound.

Varying extension to the point of absolute silence is of course used for achieving effects of subjective sound. The suppression of ambient sounds can create the sense that we are entering into the mind of a character absorbed by her or his personal story. A good example occurs in the scene in Bob Fosse's *All That Jazz* where the protagonist has a heart attack.

POINT OF AUDITION

Spatial and Subjective Point of Audition

The notion of a point of audition is a particularly tricky and ambiguous one. Several scholars (François Jost in particular) have approached this subject, and I myself devoted a chapter to it in *Le Son au cinéma*—where, to tell the truth, I raised more questions than I provided answers. It might be useful to return to it here with greater precision.

Let us first note that critics have come up with the concept of a point of audition based on the model of point of view. Here begins the problem, since cinematic point of view can refer to two different things, not always related:

1. The place from which I the spectator see; from what spatial location the scene is presented—from above, from below, from the ceiling, from inside a refrigerator. This is the strictly *spatial* designation of the term.

2. Which character in the story is (apparently) seeing what I see. This is the *subjective* designation.

In most shots of a modern-day film the camera's point of view is not that of a specific character. Which does not mean that it is necessarily arbitrary: it tends to obey certain laws and constraints. For example, the camera will rarely be located where the eye of a normal human character couldn't be (on the ceiling, in a closet, etc.). Or it only shoots along certain privileged axes, excluding others (e.g., Bergman's *After the Rehearsal*, which takes place on a theater stage, excludes the fourth side, which is the auditorium, the theater seats).

The notion of point of view in this first spatial sense rests on the possibility of inferring fairly precisely the position of an "eye" based on the image's composition and perspective.

Let us recall too that point of view in the subjective sense may be a pure effect of editing. If I cut from a shot of a character looking out the window to a shot of an exterior scene, it is highly likely that the second shot will be perceived as the character's point of view, as long as the information in shot B doesn't contradict anything in shot A.

Now, by comparison, let us examine the notion of a point of audition. This too can have two meanings, not necessarily related:

1. A spatial sense: from where do I hear, from what point in the space represented on the screen or on the soundtrack?

2. A subjective sense: which character, at a given moment of the story, is (apparently) hearing what I hear?

In the first definition, we should start by noting that the specific nature of aural perception prevents us, in most cases, from inferring a point of audition in space based on one or more sounds. This is because of the omnidirectional nature of sound (which, unlike light, travels in many directions) and also of listening (which picks up sounds in the round), as well as of phenomena involving sound reflection.

Consider a violinist playing in the center of a large round room, her audience grouped in various places against the wall. Most of the listeners, even those standing at diametrically opposite points of the room, will hear roughly the same sound, with slight differences in reverberation. These differences, related to the acoustics of the space, are not sufficient to locate specific points of audition. Every *view* of the violinist, on the other hand, can immediately situate the point from which she is being looked at.

So it is not often possible to speak of a point of audition in the sense of a precise position in space, but rather of a place of audition, or even a zone of audition.

In the second, subjective sense of point of audition, we find the same phenomenon as that which operates for vision. It is the *visual* representation of a character in closeup that, in simultaneous association with the hearing of sound, identifies this sound as being heard by the character shown.[15]

The classic example of audiovisual counterpoint cited in Eisenstein's manifesto—the image of a man on lookout duty, and the creaking of a character's boots offscreen—is of the type that is commonplace today. The question is not what characteristics of distance, color, and reverberation *in terms of sound* allow us to infer that the sound is heard by character X. For it is the image that always creates the point of audition, which in this case is worthy of the term *point*.

A special case of point of audition is one defined by sounds that "don't carry," supposedly of such a nature that one must be right up close in order to hear them. Upon hearing these sounds or indices of proximity (e.g., breathing in a voice), the spectator can locate the point of audition as that of a character in the scene—provided of course that the image, the editing and the acting all confirm the spectator's hunch. Phone conversations are the most common example. When the spectator hears the voice of the unseen person speaking clearly in sound closeup, with its characteristic filtering, she or he can identify the point of audition as being that of the character seen receiving the call. Unless, of course, we are in a situation of on-the-air, which unhooks the sound from its point of departure or arrival and accordingly renders the notion of point of audition no longer pertinent.

Frontal Voice, Back Voice

In some special cases it is nevertheless possible to attribute a direction to what is heard. A sound's high frequencies actually travel in a more directional manner than the low; and when someone speaks to us with his back turned we perceive fewer of the voice's high harmonics and find the voice less present. We can therefore speak of an audible difference between the *frontal voice* and the *back voice*.

In certain films shot in direct sound we can hear variations in a voice's color, due to the fact that a character turns away now and then from the microphone, which is generally above his head. These fluctuations in tone color help to give a particular kind of life to direct sound, and they also function as "materializing indices" (see chapter 5).

Note, however, that, first, there is no law against simulating or reconstituting such variations during postsynchronization, by moving the actor or the mike. (See for example the postsynch of *L'Homme blessé* by Patrice Chéreau.) Second, conversely, the mike during shooting can be arranged so as to follow the actor constantly "in front," particularly when the actor wears a lavaliere mike.

If the cinema usually employs the frontal voice, with the most treble allowed by the equipment, it is for a reason: high frequencies are crucial for intelligibility.

However, when the spectator hears a back voice, he or she cannot automatically infer the shot's point of audition from this: for one thing because in most cases this is a momentary effect, not stable and pronounced enough. For another, the spectator does not associate the point of audition with any mental representation of a microphone.

Blind Spots in Theorizing the Mike/Ear

This important question of the "scotomization" of the role of the microphone applies not only to the voice but also more generally to all sounds in a film.[16] And not only to the cinema but equally to most radiophonic, musical, and audiovisual creations that rely on sound recording. The camera, though excluded from the visual field, is nonetheless an active character in films, a character the spectator is aware of; but the mike must remain excluded not only from the visual and auditory field (microphone noises, etc.) but also from the spectator's very *mental representation*. It remains excluded, of course, because everything in movies, including films shot in direct sound, has been designed to this end. This naturalist perspective remains attached to sound, but it is a perspective from which the image—60s and 70s theories on the "transparency" of mise-en-scène notwithstanding—has long been liberated. The naturalist conception of sound continues to infuse real experience and critical discourse so completely that it has remained unnoticed by those who have referred to it and critiqued this same transparency on the level of the image.

We might locate the reasons for such a difference of status between image and sound, in different technical, aesthetic, physiological, and ideological problems, by asking which ones serve as alibis or coverups for which others. We must, for example, explore the implications of the fact that the ears are not disposed directionally like the eyes. Or the technical possibility, unexplored in the image but utilized in soundtracks since the coming of sound, of *mixing* sounds recorded simultaneously by several mikes placed at different locations: what becomes of the mike/ear then?

But perhaps this is beside the point. After all, the camera has little to do with our eyes (to begin with, it is monocular), which hasn't prevented it from becoming the agent of the look. So the problem lies rather in ways of thinking. To disengage sound thinking and its technical and aesthetic applications from its naturalist rut might well take many years. A concern which lies at the heart of our project.

FIVE

THE REAL AND THE

RENDERED

. . .

THE ILLUSION OF UNITY

A common perspective to which we made reference in the preceding chapter, which might be called naturalist, postulates that sounds and images start out in "natural harmony." Proponents of this approach seem surprised not to find it working in the cinema; they attribute the lack of this natural audiovisual harmony to technical falsifications in the filmmaking process. If people would only use the sounds recorded during shooting, without trying to improve on them, the argument goes, this unity could be found.

Such is of course rarely the case in reality. Even with so-called direct sound, sounds recorded during filming have always been enriched by later addition of sound effects, room tone, and other sounds. Sounds are also eliminated during the very shooting process by virtue of placement and directionality of microphones, soundproofing, and so on. In other words, the processed food of location sound is most often skimmed of certain substances and enriched with others. Can we hear a great ecological cry—"give us organic sound without additives"?

Occasionally filmmakers have tried this, like Straub in *Trop tôt trop tard*.[1] The result is totally strange. Is this because the spectator isn't accustomed to it? Surely. But also because reality is one thing, and its transposition into audiovisual two-dimensionality (a flat image and usually a monaural soundtrack), which involves radical sensory reduction, is another. What's amazing is that it works at all in this form. Indeed, we tend to forget that the audiovisual tableau of reality the cinema furnishes us, however refined it may seem, remains strictly (on the level of reproduction) that which a sketched representation of a human, with a circle for the head and sticks for the arms and legs, is to an anatomical drawing by Albrecht Dürer. There is really no reason for audiovisual relationships thus transposed to appear the same to us as they are in reality, and especially for the original sound to ring true.

We might go far as to say that all the conventions of rendering, sound effects, and so forth, which we shall examine further on, consist of accommodations and adjustments, taking into account the audiovisual transposition in order to try to conserve a certain sense of realism and truth in their new representational context.

This does not mean that it is wrong to aspire to a better simulacrum. Quite to the contrary, an experiment like Douglas Trumbull's *Showscan*, which not only uses high-definition 70-millimeter film but also considerably improves on frames per second—sixty rather than the usual flickering of twenty-four—such experiments should be taken seriously. Trompe-l'oeil, as well as "trompe-l'oreille," is a worthy art (even though the notion of trompe-l'oeil does not really involve the exact reproducing of an impression in the same way).

But when we say in disappointment that "the sound and image don't go together well," we should not blame it exclusively on the inferior quality of the reproduction of reality. For this situation merely echoes a phenomenon we are generally blind to. In concrete experience itself, independent from cinema, they sometimes don't go together either.

The most familiar example is the "mismatch" of an individual's voice and face when we have had the experience of getting to know one of them well before discovering the other. We never fail to be surprised, even shocked, when we complete the picture. Consider also the children's books that teach the noises animals make: as if there were the slightest connection, aside from the connection created by purely Pavlovian training, between the sound a duck makes and what it looks like, or the onomatopoetic words for the duck's call in different languages.

Basically, this question of the unity of sound and image would have no importance if it didn't turn out, through numerous films and numerous theories, to be the very signifier of the question of human unity, cinematic unity, unity itself. The proof is dualistic films based on a carefully planned de-acousmatization . . . which is often eluded at the last minute.[2] It is not I but the cinema that, via films like *Psycho* and *India Song*, tells us the impossible and desired meeting of sound and image can be an important thing.

Strangely, the disjunctive and autonomist impulse that predominates in intellectual discourse on the question ("wouldn't it be better if sound and image were independent?") arises entirely from the unitary illusion we have described: the false unity this thinking denounces in the current cinema implicitly suggests a true unity existing elsewhere.

Also, disjunctive ideology usually takes as given the technical fidelity of the recording. Fidelity, of course, is a problematic notion from the start.

QUESTIONS OF SOUND REPRODUCTION

A sound recording's *definition*, in technical terms, is its acuity and precision in rendering of detail. Definition is a function of the width of the frequency band (which allows us to hear frequencies all the way from extreme low to extreme high) as well as its dynamic range (amplitude of contrasts, from the weakest levels to the strongest). It is particularly through gains in high frequencies that sound has progressed in definition; high frequencies reveal a new multitude of details and information, contributing to an effect of greater presence and realism.

I am speaking of *definition* (a precise and quantifiable technical property, just like definition or sharpness in a photographic or video image) and not of *fidelity*. The latter is a tricky term; strictly speaking it would require making a continuous close comparison between the original and its reproduction, which normally would be quite difficult to physically arrange. Someone who listens to an orchestra on a sound system in his living room is not likely to be able to compare it with some orchestra playing at his doorstep. It should be known, in fact, that the notion of high fidelity is a purely commercial one, and corresponds to nothing precise or verifiable.

However, it happens that today *definition is* (mistakenly) *taken as proof of fidelity*, when it's not being confused with fidelity itself.

In the "natural" world sounds have many high frequencies that so-called hi-fi recordings do capture and reproduce better than they used to. On the other hand, current practice dictates that a sound recording should have more treble than would be heard in the real situation (for example when it's the voice of a person at some distance with back turned). No one complains of nonfidelity from too much definition! This proves that it's definition that counts for sound, and its hyperreal effect, which has little to do with the experience of direct audition. For the sake of rigor, therefore, we must speak of high definition and not high fidelity.

In the cinema sound definition is an important means of expression with multiple consequences. First, a more defined sound, containing more information, is able to provide more *materializing indices*. And second, it lends itself to a more lively, spasmodic, rapid, alert mode of listening, particularly to agile phenomena that occur in the higher frequencies (e.g., a feeling of temporal acceleration, very distinct in recent films).

Isolation and Disconnection of Sound Properties: The Example of THX

Everyone over the age of thirty today has intense memories of certain film viewing experiences; for me it was our weekly screenings at boarding school in the small town of Creil. Very eclectic programming—from American and Russian war films to low-budget westerns, with Italian neorealist films thrown in between—characterized these 16-millimeter screenings, which took place in the high school's assembly hall. Two strong aural memories stay with me. One is the wavering sound—especially noticeable during musical passages—caused by the projector's uneven speed. The other is a cavernous resonance, owing to the poor quality of sound reproduction, but also because of the reverberation that the room's acoustics gave to the actors' voices. These conditions, which we might call caricatural, were hardly more than a slight exaggeration of the conditions under which most movies were seen in those days.

Whoever goes to a modern theater graced with the label THX (created by George Lucas) will find the exact opposite: stable sound, extremely well defined in high frequencies, powerful in volume, with superb dynamic contrasts, and also, despite its strength and the probably large theater space, a sound that does not seem very reverberant at all. One finds in THX theaters the realization of the modern ideal of a great "dry" strength.

New movie houses whose acoustics are conceived or over-hauled with luxury sound projection in mind have indeed merci-lessly vanquished reverb through the choice of building materials and architectural planning. The result is that the sound feels very present and very neutral, but suddenly one no longer has the feel-ing of the real dimensions of the room, no matter how big it is. So what results is the enlargement, without any modification in tone, of a good home stereo sound.

At the start of each show some of these movie theaters play a short that consists of a title reminding you that "you are in a THX theater," during which you hear an electronic sound effect for about thirty seconds: a bunch of glissandi falling toward the low bass register, spiraling spatially around the room from speaker to speaker, ending triumphantly on an enormous chord. And it's all at an overwhelming volume that leads the audience instinctively to react by applauding in a sort of physical release.

We may note two characteristics of this sound demo that typi-fy current taste. First, the bass sound that the glissando ends on is clean of all distortion and secondary vibrations, even though very low sounds in the real world have the necessary consequence of causing small objects to vibrate—for example, a passing semi truck sets the furniture or the dishes to shaking. What the demo short is doing to stir the audience's admiration, far from any idea of fidelity, is showing off the technical capacity to isolate and purify the sound ingredients. Second, one finds no trace in the demo of the reverberation that normally accompanies and muddles loud sounds in an enclosed space.

In "real life" audio characteristics always vary in association with each other: if the volume of a sound event increases, the sound changes nature, color, resonance. In the sonic world before electronic amplification the presence of reverb prolonging the sound marked a change in spatial properties, just as the presence of secondary vibrations from the principal sound signaled a change to greater intensity. Here, on the contrary, volume aside (volume too has become a sound property as isolated or independent as others), the sound event remains as clear and distinct as if we heard it on the small speaker of a compact home stereo. So that in the type of sound projection preferred today in movie houses, where the real size of the auditorium is immaterial, amplification no longer has a true scale of reference. Amplified sound remains the same at all volume levels, without any traits that might mark the crossing of a threshold. The big THX theaters no longer give us collective sound in the old style; it's inflated personal stereo sound.

Phonogeny and Technical Mediation

The sound media (recording, talking pictures, radio) of the twenties through forties subscribed to a certain notion we have virtually forgotten today: phonogeny. Phonogeny refers to to the rather mysterious propensity of certain voices to sound good when recorded and played over loudspeakers, to inscribe themselves in the record grooves better than other voices, in short to make up for the absence of the sound's real source by means of another kind of presence specific to the medium.

This notion rose to great popularity when sound engineers of the first talkies, men who came from the recording and radio industries (from where else could they have come?), attempted to valorize phonogenic criteria, decreeing that actor X had a terrific voice while actor Y was deplorably unphonogenic. Pagnol recounts one of the best-known examples of these dangerous verdicts: during the shooting of *Marius* a Western Electric engineer declared Raimu's voice impossible to record! Not that sound engineers were always mistaken in this regard; many actors of the era were afraid they might not have the accursed phonogeny it took to survive in the age of the microphone.

Obviously this notion arose from the technical conditions that prevailed at the time: the equipment was less sensitive and precise than that of today. So certain voices did have timbres favored by the technology. They articulated themselves clearly through the microphone's filter; in a word, they "meshed" well with the sensitive part of the system.

In retrospect we might say that the voices of a Gérard Depardieu or Catherine Deneuve wouldn't have been judged phonogenic enough according to the criteria of those days: not clearly pronounced enough or sonorous enough.[3] (The verdict on Raimu, someone who surely didn't lack resonance, doubtless came from the fact that he had *too much*.) In this sense, the idea of phonogeny was nothing other than the idea of the adaptability of a certain type of voice and diction to the technical conditions of recording and reproduction. Which was by no means absurd. But even then the term also carried a strongly irrational charge. One said of a voice that it was phonogenic the way we say someone is cool or sexy, referring to some ineffable impact on people in terms of communication or seductiveness.

The criterion of phonogeny emerged, of course, as an analogy of photogeny, which was strongly operative during the era of movie stars. Unlike the former, the latter has survived to our day, and it is not uncommon to see filmmakers declare of a woman that she is not beautiful but incredibly photogenic. But the equivalent notion for sounds and the voice in particular has completely died out.

So it all seems as if we're implicitly convinced that the means of sound collection and reproduction has become transparent, rendering unnecessary any advance screening for "recordability" of a sound from the acoustic event to playback. In this, of course, we are mistaken. The most highly perfected digital recordings are certainly quantitatively richer in detail than those of yesteryear, but they are no less colored by the technical process—perhaps even more so. We simply need ten or twenty years to elapse before we can perceive this.

People who once talked about phonogeny (even if the aim of their discourse was to blindly apply the notion and issue verdicts that history would later prove wrong) were therefore actually more conscious than we are: they understood that the sound heard at the end of the process is the product of a preexisting reality plus conditions of reproduction. This end product is a specific reality: neither the neutral transmission of a sound event, nor an entire fabrication by technical means.

This leads us to wonder what the disappearance of the notion of phonogeny is the symptom of. Perhaps it signals an important mutation, to our total everyday immersion in *mediated acoustical reality* (sound is relayed by amplifiers and loudspeakers). The new sound reality has no difficulty supplanting unmediated acoustical reality in strength, presence, and impact, and bit by bit it is becoming the standard form of listening. It's a form of listening that is no longer perceived as a reproduction, as an image (with all this usually implies in terms of loss and distortion of reality), but as a more direct and immediate contact with the event. When an image has more presence than reality it tends to substitute for it, even as it denies its status of image.

Let us imagine that in our everyday visual experience certain things were to appear in windows and on screens with incomparably more vivid color, brightness, and definition than what we perceive directly. Then reality seen with the "naked eye"—with no technical mediation—would become lifeless, ill-defined, distant. This is exactly the impression felt by people at a harpsichord concert who know this instrument only from recordings or radio: "You can't hear a thing!"

Curiously, the more unmediated acoustical reality loses its value as real experience and the less it is the lived standard to which we compare what we hear, the more it becomes the abstract reference we call on conceptually—for example, regarding the notion of acoustic fidelity that the cinema demands. The more we use recorded and/or transmitted sound, the more we mythify its contrary: a natural acoustical experience that we actually have less and less frequently.

The fading of the idea of phonogeny has another origin as well. Phonogeny still had meaning in an era during which people had learned to speak and to project their voices in a predominantly mechanical environment. Today, the manner in which people speak is just as strongly influenced by voices heard on television, radio, and films as by voices heard "naturally"; in this environment it is difficult to compare a natural voice to a mediated one. For natural voices are not only produced but also heard by unconscious comparison with mediated ones, which tend to stand out more. It is also in light of this new fact of our experience that the notion of phonogeny needs to be rethought—but first, rediscovered.

Silences of Direct Sound

Many people consider *location sound* not only the sole morally acceptable solution in filmmaking but also the one that simplifies everything, since it eliminates the problem of having to make choices. Rohmer's films are mentioned most often when critics wish to vaunt the virtues of location sound and to present it as a simple, obvious, rigorous, and irresistible option. However, Rohmer's choices for direct sound consciously involve sacrifices and difficulties. The location sound is subjugated to the artist's purposes. In the acoustic climate of *The Aviator's Wife*, for example, shot in Paris on location, we notice a great neutrality, and an almost complete silence of the setting. There is nothing to disturb our concentration on the characters and their lines. All events that usually intrude on sound recording in a city or in the country have been completely eliminated, but the life that can come with them has also been eliminated in the process.

When Philippe Marlaud and then Mathieu Carrière go up the stairs leading to Marie Rivière's little gabled apartment at the beginning of the film, we hear no sound but their footsteps. When Marie Rivière opens her windows we hear an anonymous hum of the city, very general and diffused, through the windows. . . . And when characters speak in her bedroom nothing gets in the way of their lines, even though Lord knows how many intrusions occur in a real apartment in the city.

It seems obvious that Rohmer in his soundtracks sniffs out and chases away any anecdotal sound—whether it's the kind that's recorded accidentally by the location mike, such as beeps and honks, sirens, shouts, or other noises, or whether it's the kind of anecdotal sound usually added intentionally later in the mix, in accordance with certain codes, habits, and clichés. For example, for going up the stairs, Rohmer could have put stairwell noises and radio sounds to suggest the time of day, 7:00 A.M. When Marie Rivière opens her windows, many films set in Paris normally mix in the cooing of pigeons to complete the picture, to flesh out the city and its rooftops, and to enliven the soundtrack with a conventional decorative touch. Likewise, in Rohmer's film, when Philippe Marlaud walks down the street his footsteps are heard in an indistinct hum of traffic; no specific noise, no burst of conversation comes to break the atmosphere. The risk of a spontaneous intrusion of sound when you film with location sound is that it might give a sudden specific and undesired meaning to a word of dialogue or to an actor's gesture. A motorscooter accelerating offscreen, a radio or TV whose sound comes through the windows might not just drown out the actor's line but inflect it, make it mean something else.

And this is precisely the risk that Straub and Huillet accepted the run of in *Othon*, when a backfiring motorcycle almost grotesquely accentuated a line of Corneille. In general, however, the filmmakers chose shooting locations that were sufficiently removed from traffic, so the traffic for the most part consisted of a continuous generalized hum.

In *The Aviator's Wife*, in order to obtain this well-blended sonic environment with nothing standing out, this environmental silence enveloping the characters (also very noticeable in the long sequence shot in the park at Les Buttes-Chaumont), Rohmer had to shoot at precise hours in the day (which by no means always matched the supposed time of the action), and to reject any takes marred by interruptions. In a word, it was only through a process of choice and elimination that Rohmer could construct the sonic milieu he envisioned. Thus, the notion of direct sound involves no less of a reconstruction (even if by simple subtraction) than the notion of postsynchronized sound.

The most noticeable and anecdotal sound in this film is Marie's sink vibrating when she turns on the faucet. Even this noise was not introduced or kept on the soundtrack for any purely comical or picturesque effect in itself. It has a precise function in the screenplay: a suitor uses the necessary repairs in her apartment as a pretext to plague this young woman (who will continue to reject him). Besides, the noise does not go unnoticed; Mathieu Carrière refers to it directly. It is thus integrated into the dialogue, digested by the screenplay.

The risk of direct sound and location shooting is that unplanned visuals and sounds that are not integrated in the fabric of the screenplay can intrude, take on an autonomous existence. Some filmmakers love and even provoke such intrusions; others go so far as to simulate them. Still others avoid them: even Godard's work allows no anecdotal intrusion of sound to distract from his aims. Thus, direct sound is not so "open," not so synonymous with "simple and obvious" solutions as it may seem.

Sound Truth and Sound Verisimilitude

A fourth question regarding sound reality, the question of verisimilitude, is a terribly ambiguous and complicated one. Let us merely examine several aspects of it.

First of all, sound that rings true for the spectator and sound that *is* true are two very different things. In order to assess the truth of a sound, we refer much more to codes established by cinema itself, by television, and narrative-representational arts in general, than to our hypothetical lived experience. Besides, quite often we have no personal memory we might refer to regarding a scene we see. If we are watching a war film or a storm at sea, what idea did most of us actually have of sounds of war or the high seas before hearing the sounds in the films?

And in the case of scenes we might experience in everyday life (with Rohmer, for example), hardly ever have we paid distinct and focused attention to these sounds either. We only retain impressions of such sounds if they carry material and emotional significance; those that don't interest or surprise us get eliminated from memory. Everyday reality hardly puts us in a position to listen to its sounds for themselves and to focus on their intrinsic acoustical qualities, since context so strongly influences our perception. In order to really listen to sounds one would have to recreate the auditory analogy of the visual *camera obscura* that allowed painters to observe nature and to apprehend its true values of light and color.

The codes of theater, television, and cinema have created very strong conventions, determined by a concern for the *rendering* more than for literal truth. We are all thoroughly familiar with these conventions, and they easily override our own experience and substitute for it, becoming our reference for reality itself.

For one thing, film as a recording art has developed specific codes of realism that are related to its own technical nature. Of two war reports that come back from a very real war, the one in which the image is shaky and rough, with uneven focus and other "mistakes," will seem more true than the one with impeccable framing, perfect visibility, and imperceptible grain. In much the same way for sound, the impression of realism is often tied to a feeling of discomfort, of an uneven signal, of interference and microphone noise, etc. These effects can of course be simulated in the studio during postproduction and orchestrated: *Alien*, for example, uses effects of acoustic discomfort to heighten its sense of realism.

For another thing, when the spectator hears a so-called realistic sound, he is not in a position to compare it with the real sound he might hear if he were standing in that actual place. Rather, in order to judge its "truth," the spectator refers to his memory of this type of sound, a memory resynthesized from data that are not solely acoustical, and that is itself influenced by films.

Naturally criteria for auditory verisimilitude differ according to the specific competences and experience of the individual. A nature lover wrote a letter to the editor of *Télérama* (France's *TV Guide*), having seen Bertrand Blier's *Trop belle pour toi*. He expressed shock in hearing birds that in his experience cannot sing either in the season in which the story takes place (winter) nor in the location shown (the area of Béziers). This evidence exposed the fabricated nature of the soundtrack and its trumped-up sound effects, and prevented him from "believing" the scene.

Let us note that this demand for realism has its blind spots and limitations. For one thing, it is altogether conceivable that through a fluke of nature the birds in question really were singing during the shooting. For another, the same spectator who's finicky about sounds might be indifferent to aberrant light (incoherent lighting setups given the light sources depicted) that might disturb the photography specialist. In other words, every film is premised on the the acceptance of rules of the game—not the least of which is agreeing to see flat images in depth!

RENDERING AND REPRODUCTION

What Is a Rendering?

In considering the realist and narrative function of diegetic sounds (voices, music, noise), we must distinguish between the notions of *rendering* and *reproduction*. The film spectator recognizes sounds to be truthful, effective, and fitting not so much if they reproduce what would be heard in the same situation in reality, but if they render (convey, express) the feelings associated with the situation. This occurs at a barely conscious level, for filmviewers (in which we must include most critics and theoreticians) have little more than a fairly crude and immediate understanding of the cinema's figurative nature.

Leonardo da Vinci made a remark in his *Notebooks* that synthesizes the problem quite well: "If a man jumps on the points of his feet, his weight does not make any sound."[4] Here we have the creator of the Mona Lisa stating with wonderment that sound does not render a person's weight, as if it had a special vocation to do so. In other words, the assumption is that a sound should constitute a microcosm of the whole event, with the same characteristics of speed, matter, and expression. Everyone continues to have this same expectation of sound, centuries after Leonardo, despite the recordings of acoustical reality that can be made today, which should disabuse us of our misconceptions.

In truth the question is a complex one, even at the very level of language. Consider a scene in Truffaut's *The Bride Wore Black*. Claude Rich plays a recording for his friend Jean-Claude Brialy in which we can hear a subtle sound of some kind of friction, unidentifiable and periodic. It leaves Brialy perplexed—he can't tell what it is. Rich then identifies the sound as that of a woman's stockings as she crosses her legs. He specifies that it was recorded without the knowledge of the woman in question. He adds that the lady was wearing nylons: "I tried it with silk stockings, but that didn't give a good rendering at all." What does he mean by "rendering," this character presented to us as a ladies' man?

If I understand correctly, in playing his recording the character was not so interested in getting his friend to identify the real source. If he were, he could have said, "But you couldn't tell that it was the sound of stockings." Rather, he wished to convey an effect or feeling associated with the sound source—an effect of sensuality, eroticism, intimacy, contact. This is why the nylon stockings, even though a more common material, proved more to his taste than silk stockings in the rendering of the recording.

The pleasure-seeker played by Claude Rich conducted an experiment demonstrating that a sound doesn't necessarily "render" its source: silk does not make a noise that self-evidently relates the sensuality, the luxury, and the tactile pleasure of silk.

But he also demonstrated (without articulating the consequences) that the noise of nylon stockings itself needs to be accompanied by a verbal explanation in order to become evocative, i.e., to give a "rendering." Truffaut himself must have reached this conclusion when he faced the problem of producing the sound we hear in the film (which is no doubt the work of a Foley artist).

Thus we can say that in this filmic example one of the two lessons of the experiment—that the nylons give a better rendering than the silk stockings—overshadows the other—that in order to refer to their source, both sounds need to be identified verbally. One blots out the other, rather than the two mutually indicating each other or dispelling the common illusion out of which both arise—the illusion of a natural narrativity of sounds.

So common belief lends a double property to sound: not only do we believe that sound can "objectively" and single-handedly indicate its source but also that it evokes impressions linked to this source. For example, of the sound of a caress we normally say that skin is rubbing on skin, and also we say it with sensuality, and not clinically. This is really magical thinking, as when it is believed that making an image of a person takes away his or her soul.

In a scene in *Children of a Lesser God* William Hurt questions his deaf-mute lover, who is reading his lips and gestures. Consumed with curiosity about what she must be feeling, he asks her what a sound she can't hear is like—for example, what does a wave sound like? Her answer is to run her open hands along her own body, miming a caress. He, in love (but also obsequious toward the deaf), says, enraptured, that yes, that's what waves sound like. Even though what Marlee Matlin was miming had nothing at all to do with the sound of waves, but rather described the wave in general, or rather the wave-and-my-body.

What Is Rendered Is a Clump of Sensations

Why is this so, and why should sounds "render" their sources all by themselves—a belief that sound-effects people are obviously completely disabused of? No doubt because sounds are neither experienced objectively nor named, and through a magnetism related to all the vagueness and uncertainty surrounding them, sounds "attract" affects for which they are not especially responsible.[5]

It might be believed that the question of rendering boils down to that of translating one order of sensation into another. For example, in Truffaut's sequence, rendering would involve "transliterating" tactile sensations into auditory sensations: the rustling of nylon stockings would have to render the touch of legs sheathed in silk.

But in reality rendering involves perceptions that belong to no sensory channel in particular. When Leonardo da Vinci marveled that sound does not render the fall of a human body, he was thinking not only about the body's weight but also its mass as well as the sensation of falling, the jolt it causes to the person falling, and so forth. In other words, he was thinking about something that cannot be reduced to one simple sensory message. This is surely why, in most films that show falling, we are given to hear (in contradiction to real-life experience) great crashes whose volume has the duty of "rendering" weight, violence, and pain.

In fact, most of our sensory experiences consist of these clumps of agglomerated sensations.

It is morning; I open the shutters of my bedroom window. All at once I am hit with images that stun me, a violent sensation of light on my corneas, the heat of the sun if it's a nice day out, and outdoor noises that get louder as the shutters open. All this comes upon me as a whole, not dissociated into separate elements.

I have already cited in *La Toile trouée* the example of the car that zooms by while you stand on the curb: your sudden impression is composed of the sound that comes from a distance and takes a certain amount of time to disappear once the car has passed, the perception of a vibration of the ground, the vehicle's path across your field of vision, sensations of air movement, changes in temperature, and so on.

On screen, the audiovisual channel has to do all the work of transmitting these two scenes: the filmmaker must "render" them by the sole means of image and sound. Sound especially will be called upon to render the situation's violence and suddenness. In the *lived experience* of these two sample scenes, the changes in volume when we open the shutters or when the car rushes by are progressive and relative, even modest. In any case they're not surprising: before opening the window or seeing the car, we already hear their sounds. But the cinema systematically exaggerates the contrast of intensity. This device of exaggerating contrast is a kind of white lie committed even in films that use direct sound. Sometimes a sound will be made to arise suddenly out of complete silence, at the exact moment of the window-opening or the car's passing. The point is that the sound here must tell the story of a whole a rush of composite sensations and not just the auditory reality of the event.

This issue of rendering illustrates certain problems in representation—pictoral problems in the classical sense—largely ignored by film analysis, which has taken the cinema's figurative dimension as something settled and agreed upon. In sidestepping the difficulties such analysis of course has a much easier task; it can move directly on to the *terra firma* of narratological problems, territory already well scouted by literary studies.

If for our part we consider these questions to be important— not without shocking some of our students—it is because we believe that in addressing them the cinema, reproblematizing itself as a simulacrum, can find new vitality.

Materializing Sound Indices (M.S.I.)

A sound of voices, noise, or music has a particular number of *materializing sound indices*, from zero to infinity, whose relative abundance or scarcity always influences the perception of the scene and its meaning. Materializing indices can pull the scene toward the material and concrete, or their sparsity can lead to a perception of the characters and story as ethereal, abstract and fluid.

The materializing indices are the sound's details that cause us to "feel" the material conditions of the sound source, and refer to the concrete process of the sound's production. They can give us information about the substance causing the sound—wood, metal, paper, cloth—as well as the way the sound is produced—by friction, impact, uneven oscillations, periodic movement back and forth, and so on. Among the most common noises surrounding us there are some that are poor in materializing indices, which, when heard apart from their source (acousmatized), become enigmas: a motor noise or creaking can acquire an abstract quality, deprived of referentiality.

In many musical traditions perfection is defined by an absence of m.s.i.s. The musician's or singer's goal is to purify the voice or instrument sound of all noises of breathing, scratching, or any other adventitious friction or vibration linked to producing the musical tone. Even if she takes care to conserve at least an exquisite hint of materiality and noise in the release of the sound, the musician's effort lies in detaching the latter from its causality. Other musical cultures—some African traditions, for example—strive for the opposite: the "perfect" instrumental or vocal performance enriches the sound with supplementary noises, which bring out rather than dissimulate the material origin of the sound. From this contrast we see that the composite and culture-bound notion of *noise* is closely related to the question of materializing indices.

The apportioning of materializing sound indices is controlled either at the source, by the ways in which noises are produced during filming as well as how they are recorded, or during mixing and in postsynchronization. In the audiovisual contract the way m.s.i.s are apportioned plays a preeminent part in mise-en-scène, dramatization, and the film's structuration.

A sound of a footstep, for example, can contain a minimum of materializing sound indices (abstract footstep sounds like the unobtrusive clicking in serial TV dramas) or, on the contrary, many details of texture, giving the impression of leather and cloth, and cues about the composition of what is being walked on—gravel crunching, a squeaking wood floor. Either option may be chosen in connection with any image, and synchresis predisposes the spectator to hear either one and accept the sounds he hears. At the beginning of *Mon Oncle* when the Arpel family gets up in the morning, the little boy's footsteps on the cement in the yard make a pleasant and concrete rustling, while those of his father, a large, uptight, and unhappy man, only produce a thin, unrealistic "ding."

Materializing sound indices frequently consist of *unevennesses* in the course of a sound that denote a resistance, breach, or hitch in the movement or the mechanical process producing the sound. An m.s.i. in a voice might also consist of the presence of breathing noise, mouth and throat sounds, but also any changes in timbre (if the voice breaks, goes off-key, is scratchy). For the sound of a musical instrument, m.s.i.s would include the attack of a note, unevennesses, friction, breaths, and fingernails on piano keys. An out of tune chord in a piano piece or uneven voicing in a choral piece have a materializing effect on the sound heard. They return the sound to the sender, so to speak, in accentuating the work of the sound's emitter and its faults instead of allowing us to forget the emitter in favor of the sound or the note itself.

In the communion mass in *Le Plaisir* Ophuls sets up a contrast between the very materialized vocalizing of the priests (very dense, throaty, off-key voices) and the faultless and pure voices of the little communicants. We don't even see the children singing, unlike the officiants from whose crude perspiring faces we are not spared.

Take one image and compare the effect of a music cue played on a well-tuned piano with the effect of a cue played on a slightly out of tune piano with a few bad keys. We tend to read the first cue more readily as "pit music," while with the second, even if the instrument isn't identified or shown in the image, we will sense its concrete presence in the setting.

The effects of spatial acoustics (the sensation of distance between sound source and microphone and the presence of a characteristic reverberation that exposes the sound as produced in a concrete space) can also contribute toward materializing sound. But not systematically: for a certain type of unrealistic reverberation, not commensurate with the place shown in the image, can also be coded as dematerializing and symbolizing.

Reinforcement with materializing indices (or, on the other hand, erasing them) contributes toward the creation of a universe, and can take on metaphysical meaning. Bresson and Tarkovsky have a predilection for materializing indices that immerse us in the here-and-now (dragging footsteps with clogs or old shoes in Bresson's films, agonized coughing and painful breathing in Tarkovsky's). Tati, by suppressing m.s.i.s, subtly gives us an ethereal perception of the world: think of the abstract, dematerialized klunk of the dining room's swinging door in *Mr. Hulot's Holiday.*

In films shot with direct sound the changes in voice color resulting from sound recording conditions (e.g., microphone placement at a person's face or back) also count as materializing indices, since they localize the voice in question in a concrete space and they anchor the sound in a more tangible quadrant of reality.

Examples of Rendering: *The Bear* and *Who Framed Roger Rabbit*

We might recall that in anticipation of the Christmas holidays the autumn 1988 movie season saw animal species temporarily steal the show from the usual human stars. On our left, there was a cartoon rabbit who chatted with real characters and became ensconced in carnal human space, projecting shadows, smashing against real walls, manipulating solid objects. This was of course Robert Zemeckis's *Who Framed Roger Rabbit*. To our right, several hundred pounds of decidedly real and endangered wildlife were framed as artfully as John Wayne or Gérard Depardieu might be, in *The Bear* by Jean-Jacques Annaud. As is customary, the publicity campaigns surrounding these two releases revealed several "secrets" about the production. Rarely, however, was there any mention of the problems that might have been involved in creating the films' soundtracks.

How, for example, did *Roger Rabbit*'s soundmen conceive of the sounds their rabbit-hero would make? Apparently—but this is only a hypothesis, based on my audio-viewing of the film—they started out with what is paradoxical about the cartoon form itself. It is graphic, ostentatiously *drawn*, but at the same time it's modeled in three dimensions, through a play of shadows and volumes added onto a basically flat nature. And they must have wondered what sounds could convincingly make this creature seem to maneuver in a concrete universe when it walked, slid, or banged into something.

In the noisy world of the traditional animated cartoon no one ever had to ask these questions. Filmmakers used stylized synch sound effects analogous to those in the circus, presenting sounds that followed the action as sonic symbols for impacts and movements without specifying what substances the moving beings were made out of. We should note that certain comedy directors like Jacques Tati and Blake Edwards have enjoyed treating humans in a similar way.

But we find the contrary in *Roger Rabbit*, whose soundtrack subtly attempts to give material solidity to a graphic being. The noises of the cartoon characters' bodies remain light, and the single moment in the film involving a sound effect designed to be consciously noticed is where the pulpy Jessica rubs up against the human detective played by Bob Hoskins. When the latter's very concrete skull bumps into the voluminous cartoon breasts, we hear a hollow clang, which never fails to get a laugh. But there are many other moments when the cartoon characters, especially Roger Rabbit, subtly make noises of friction and contact, conveying the impression of a thin hollow elastic material, like inflated plastic.

So through sound, the effects experts of *Roger Rabbit* let us know that the "toons" are hollow, lightweight beings. If the spectator pays little attention to these sounds, that doesn't mean by any stretch of the imagination that she doesn't hear them, or isn't influenced by them in her perception of the images. Watching the screen, she believes she simply sees what in fact she hears-sees, owing to the phenomenon I have described as added value.

It is not certain that the various creators and technicians who worked with Jean-Jacques Annaud on *The Bear* had such a very different plan from the creators of the American movie. Of course they had a different point of departure—real-life (trained) bears being filmed as human actors would be. Only the crew of *The Bear* knew that you can't just film shots of a bear and thereby automatically convey the bear's strength, its odor, weight, and *animality*: and they knew to draw on sound to aid in rendering all these qualities.

As we know, Annaud chose not to keep the direct sound he obtained during filming. There are obvious material reasons for such a choice, not the least of which is that the beasts could only be directed by means of profuse injunctions and vociferations from their trainers offscreen. In France, where just about everyone toots his or her horn for direct sound, most filmmakers still go ahead and partially or wholly redo sound after shooting anyway; ordinarily, though, this fact is hidden like a shameful thing. So let us give credit to Annaud for his honesty, which helped him adopt a widespread practice with few qualms. Thus we learned that the animal cries of his film had been redone in a zoo, and were to various degrees edited and sometimes even dubbed by humans—particularly the noises that help express in the baby bear's throat an entire range of anthropocentric emotions: all this under the supervision of a sound designer named Laurent Quaglio.

Another behind-the-scenes artisan who seems to have played a key part in the "rendering" of the bear was the eminent Foley artist Jean-Pierre Lelong, who recreated the animal's footsteps in the studio. He is probably responsible for the undeniable success of the first appearance of Bart, the big bear. The impression of a crushing mass results largely from the cavernous sounds we hear in synchrony with the monster's stride.

But at other moments (for example, when Bart meets the hunter), the very realism of the cinematography—i.e., true closeups rather than shots taken from a distance by telephoto lenses—makes us realize how the ferocious roaring was added on to the image afterwards so as to force the meaning. There is also a lack of naturalness in the sound mix as a whole, a muddy consistency that colors Philippe Sarde's orchestral score as well. It is hard to tell at what stage of the mixing or editing this problem was introduced. Most probably, it's one of those problems of technical coordination from which the French cinema tends to suffer.

Sound in Animation: Putting Sound to Movements

In a book on the development of musicality in children, two scholars, François Delalande and Bernadette Céleste, investigated a common yet misunderstood phenomenon. They studied the vocalizing with which children at play punctuate their movements of objects, dolls, toy cars, and so on.[6] I am not speaking of dialogues children have with their toy friends, but sound effects they produce orally to accompany these activities. Delalande and Céleste's observations on this subject are highly interesting for our own inquiry. For their research also applies to the questions involved in putting sounds into films, in particular the matter of how to do sound for cartoons and other kinds of animated film.

Delalande and Céleste determined that sometimes these vocal productions "partake in a code of expression of feelings" (the descending "ooooh" from a little girl when the toy character she's playing with gets a tear in her dress), and sometimes, particularly in boys' play, noises such as "brrrrr," "vrrrr," "bzzhhhh," and other labial and pharyngial vocalizations function as sound effects and punctuations to accompany movements of vehicles, and actions of their robots and their machines. Where can they possibly come from, these codes governing such spontaneous sound productions whose job is to bring immobile objects to life?

Delalande and Céleste attempted to map out the functions of

such vocal expressions in children. These include the "representation" of movements and dynamics of characters and machines involved in playing. Such representation is not so much in line with a strategy of literal reproduction, as in terms of a "mechanical and even mainly kinematic (movement-oriented) symbolism." The point is not to imitate the noise produced by the thing, but to evoke the thing's movement by means of isomorphism, that is, by "a similarity of movement between the sound and the movement it represents." When one of the boys they observed at play stops rolling his little car around, he makes a sliding sound with his mouth that recalls an airplane diving. "The descending part of the sound probably represents the slowing down of the vehicle." The sound here conveys movement and its trajectory rather than the timbre of the noise that supposedly issues from a car. "The substance of the sound has nothing to do with resemblance, it's the sound's trajectory that does." It is not difficult to see that this kind of relation between sound and movement is the very same relation used in the animated film, especially the cartoon.

Let us return to the famous and common procedure of using an ascending musical figure to accompany the climbing of a hill or a flight of stairs . . . even though the sounds of the character's footsteps do not themselves go up any scale of pitches. What is being imitated here is the trajectory and not the sound of the trajectory, drawing on a universal spatial symbolism of musical pitches. Sound is applied to most visual movements in this manner, and the animated film is the privileged province of this sound-image relation.

The animated film also provided the reference for *mickeymousing*, the name for a process of music-image pairing that's employed in the nonanimated cinema as well. Mickeymousing consists in following the visual action in synchrony with musical trajectories (rising, falling, zigzagging) and instrumental punctuations of action (blows, falls, doors closing). This device, which I have already mentioned in connection with *The Informer*, has been criticized for being redundant, but it has an obvious function nonetheless. Try watching a Tex Avery cartoon without the sound, especially without the musical part. Silent, the visual figures tend to telescope, they do not impress themselves well in the mind, they go by too fast. Owing to the eye's relative inertia and laziness compared to the ear's agility in identifying moving figures, sound helps to imprint rapid visual sensations into memory. Indeed, it plays a more important role in this capacity of aiding the apprehension of visual movements than in focusing on its own substance and aural density.

Many variations on this theme are possible. Take Tex Avery's *What Price Fleadom*, the story of a tender idyll between a male flea and the wandering dog who offers him shelter in his fur, until the day when a female flea, on another dog . . . you can guess the rest. The various gags and actions of the film are accompanied and punctuated by the musical figures you would expect; when the flea jumps, a music cue jumps with it, as in the circus. But sometimes, by means of diabolical touches here and there, the real and the corporeal reemerge in the soundtrack. When a big city dog crushes the flea under his heel, we hear a slight but realistic crushing sound, like the one I mentioned in *The Skin*. Disturbing. Or when the wandering dog is happy to find Homer the flea, who returns with a big family; the cartoon animal pants with pleasure at the prospect of lodging everyone, and the panting is concrete, realistic, canine. Animality in Avery's cartoons is never very far away. And sound—ineffable and elusive sound—so clear and precise in our perception of it, and at the same time so open-ended in all it can relate—infiltrates the reassuring, closed and inconsequential universe of the cartoon like a drop of reality, a tiny, anxiety-producing drop of reality.

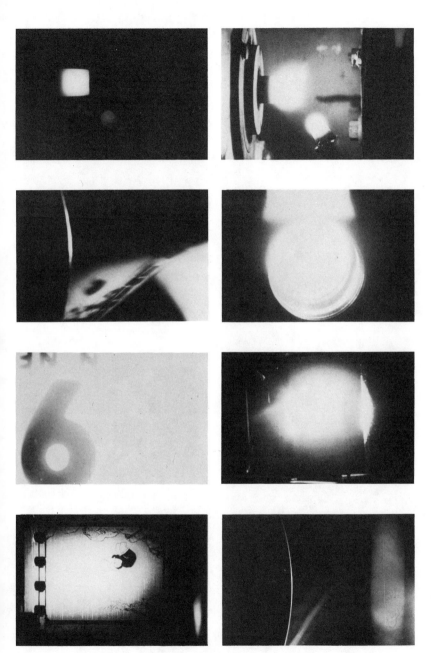

Persona (Ingmar Bergman, 1967). Stills from the prologue analyzed in chapter 10.

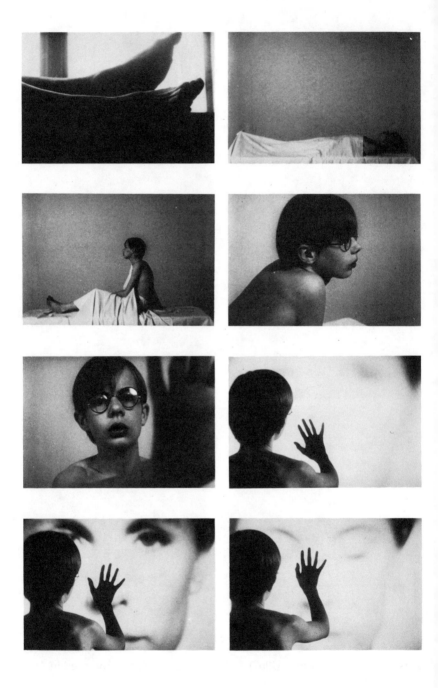

A production still from *The Invisible Man* (James Whale, 1933).

Sven Wollter, Erland Josephson, Filippa Franzen, and Susan Fleetwood in *The Sacrifice* (Andrei Tarkovsky, 1987).

Anne Brumangne, Adriano Apra, and Anthony Pensabene in *Othon*
(Jean Marie Straub and Danièle Huillet, 1969).

Marlee Matlin and William Hurt in *Children of a Lesser God*
(Randa Haines, 1987).

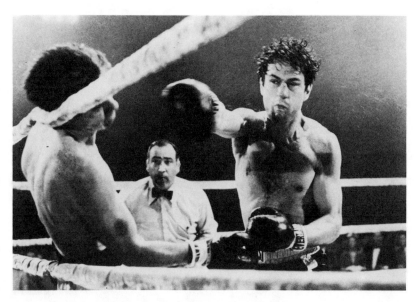

Robert DeNiro in *Raging Bull* (Martin Scorsese, 1980).

John Hurt in *Alien* (Ridley Scott, 1979).

Philippe Marlaud in *The Aviator's Wife* (Eric Rohmer, 1981).

Bob Hoskins and Jessica in *Who Framed Roger Rabbit*
(Robert Zemeckis, 1988).

SIX

PHANTOM

AUDIO-VISION

• • •

THE OTHER SIDE OF THE IMAGE

In Tarkovsky's final film, *The Sacrifice,* one can hear
sounds that already seem to come from the other side, as if they're
heard by an immaterial ear, liberated from the hurly-burly of our
human world. Sung by sweet young human voices, they seem to
be calling to us, resonating in a limpid atmosphere. They lead us
far back to childhood, to an age when it felt as if we were by
nature immortal. A spectator might hear these songs without
consciously realizing it; nothing in the image points to or engages
with them. It is as if they are the afterlife of the image, like what
we'd discover if the screen were a hill and we could go see what

was on the other side. The closing credits inform us that they are traditional Swedish songs: hardly songs, more like invocations.

This is fairly typical of the sound of Tarkovsky's feature films: it calls to another dimension, it has gone elsewhere, disengaged from the present. It can also murmur like the drone of the world, at once close and disquieting. Tarkovsky, whom some call a painter of the earth—but an earth furrowed by streams and roads like the convolutions of a living brain—knew how to make magnificent use of sound in his films: sometimes muffled, diffuse, often bordering on silence, the oppressive horizon of our life; sometimes noises of presence, cracklings, plip-plops of water. Sound is also used in wide rhythms, in vast sheets. Swallows pass over the Swedish house of *The Sacrifice* every five or ten minutes; the image never shows them and no character speaks of them. Perhaps the person who hears these bird calls is the child in the film, a reclining convalescent—someone who has all the time in the world to wait for them, to watch for them, to come to know the rhythm of their returning.

The other side of the image is also found, in *Mr. Hulot's Holiday*, in that scene at the beach where what we see—awkward vacationers, with pinched expressions and cramped gestures— finds its diametric opposite in what we hear. The soundtrack conveys playing and shouting, with excited children, in a beautiful reverb-filled texture; the sound seems to have been collected on a real visit to a bathing beach. Basically characters in the image seem annoyed and those on the soundtrack are having fun. Which, as I have already pointed out, becomes obvious only when we mask out the image. What we then discover lurking just beneath the surface is an entire world of lively adults and children, hassling and yelling to one another; though never on screen, they are much more alive than those we do see. And on the screen the film's light is flat and two-dimensional, in the indoor scenes as well as the exteriors, while the sounds of games on the beach reveal several nuanced and distinct depth planes.

So what we have here in *Mr. Hulot's Holiday* is two superimposed "ghosts," as Merleau-Ponty termed them: a ghost is the kind of perception made by only one sense.[1] (Of course, there is a part of the soundtrack—very specific sound effects—whose function is to give life to certain visual details and actions, and to give them a tangible reality on the screen.) These two ghost-universes are far from symmetrical. There is the world in the frame where we can identify things; Tati invites spectators in to point out gags to one another from our imaginary seats on the cafe terrace. Then there is the other world, that of sound, which is not named or identified. Children's or bathers' voices cry, "Go on, Robert!" or "Wow, is this water cold!" but no one in the image responds to the voices or acknowledges their existence. They literally and immediately engrave themselves in our memory, just as other phrases of this sort, registered and never named, may have imprinted themselves during childhood. One world is more ghostly than the other, and it's the world of sound.

What is the effect of this strange contrast? Does Tati's audiovisual strategy produce added value? That is, are we dealing with sound that enlivens the image, and deepens it in spatial terms? I don't think so, for in this particular case the image is not so malleable, and from the outset it contradicts the sonic environment too much.

So is it a matter of "counterpoint"? Literally speaking, yes, but counterpoint that isn't audio-viewed as such. No one ever notices or remarks on it; the ambient sounds of beach play are taken for natural atmosphere that oozes from the setting.

An effect, then, neither of added value nor counterpoint. In Tati's film as in Tarkovsky's *Sacrifice* we encounter a mysterious effect of "hollowing-out" of audiovisual form: as if audio and visual perceptions were divided one by the other instead of mutually compounded, and in this quotient another form of reality, of combination, emerged.

Thus there are in the audiovisual contract certain relationships of absence and emptiness that set the audiovisual note to vibrating in a distinct and profound way. These relationships are what the present chapter sets out to describe.

A PHANTOM BODY: THE INVISIBLE MAN

It is no coincidence that one of the greatest early sound films was the one about *The Invisible Man*. The world's oldest stories tell us of invisible men and creatures; it was to be expected that the cinema, art of illusion and conjuring, would seize upon this theme with particular relish. Méliès is probably the one who inaugurated the trend in 1904 with his *Siva l'Invisible*. This trick film was imitated by other silent films; some were adaptations of H. G. Wells's novel *The Invisible Man*, published in 1897. It is easy to see why the talkies would give a big boost to the invisible man theme; and indeed, very soon after the coming of sound James Whale's wonderful film of 1933 achieved tremendous success.

The sound film made it possible to create the character through his voice, and thereby give him a wholly new dimension and a completely different presence. In Whale's film he is rather talkative, even bombastic, as if intoxicated by the new talkies. His loquaciousness might also reflect the filmmakers' desire to give Claude Rains (who does not visibly appear until the very last shot—the rest of the time he's completely covered in clothing and bandages) some room to show off his acting.

The impact of *The Invisible Man* stems from the cinema's discovery of the powers of the invisible voice. This film is a special case: compare it to the invisible voice in a contemporaneous film like Fritz Lang's *Testament of Dr. Mabuse*. The speaking body of Wells's hero Griffin is not invisible by virtue of being offscreen or hidden behind a curtain, but apparently really *in* the image, even—and above all—when we don't see him there.

This situation has fairly humorous cinematic consequences, for example, when the camera accompanies the protagonist's ascent of a large empty staircase by means of a tilt. It's as if the camera, incapable of seeing Griffin, insists nevertheless on framing him and keeping him in the field of vision. At the same time, we understand that this camera movement is informing us that he is going upstairs; it is an index of the filmmakers' knowledge of mise-en-scène, of how to film the motion of the hero even in his very invisibility.

So Griffin is a singular form of "acousmêtre" (see below): along with the other invisible voices who would populate the sound cinema he shares certain privileges and certain powers, particularly a surprising ability to move around, to slip through the traps set for him. If he ends up caught and defeated, it's only because it snowed and his footsteps are visible in the snow as he imprints them.

Another major characteristic he shares with cinema's other invisible voices is that his downfall and death are linked to his return to the common fate of visibility. In the film's final, disconcerting image, Griffin is dying in his hospital bed; at first we can only pinpoint him by his voice and a dent in the pillow. But since the substance that hides him ceases to act when he dies, he gradually takes visual form, by means of two overlapping superimpositions. First we see a death's head appear, then it is filled in with the flesh of the face fixed forever—the face seen for the first time only when Griffin is no more. The idea comes from Wells, but the film has a beautiful way of exploiting it, by depicting a death in reverse. In the film, becoming substantial for the eye means meeting with the common fate of corruptible beings, and to leave an impression on film is to be stamped with the seal of death that film places on those it captures.

Although Griffin is invisible, the screenplay doesn't construct his body as immaterial; he can be nabbed. His invisibility is really the only trait that allows him to escape the servitude common to the human condition. He has other constraints that visible beings do not have: he must go naked when he does not want to be seen, hide in order to eat (since the food he takes in remains visible until completely digested), and so on. Everything in this character, from the disguise he must assume when he wishes to appear without giving himself away, which makes him look somewhat like a seriously wounded man, to the complaints he makes during his frequent tirades to say that he's cold or hungry or sleepy, everything shows us that what we have here is not a flying superhero but a suffering body, a "phantom" body whose organic character is accentuated rather than subtilized. Thus, when he handles objects and opens doors he demonstrates his invisibility but also makes a show of his lowly human condition of having to do everything himself, with no telekinesic power. And when he wraps himself up in a blanket to get warm, we are frightened to see that the blanket marries the contours of a nothingness, but this nothingness—which speaks—is a form that makes us feel cold.

The sound film would not often recapture the strangeness and above all the conviction with which this half-embodied voice was elaborated in *The Invisible Man*. But it did continue to develop a form of "phantom" character specific to the art of film, and to which we owe some of the greatest films of the thirties to seventies: the *acousmêtre*.

THE ACOUSMETRE

The *acousmêtre* is this acousmatic character whose relationship to the screen involves a specific kind of ambiguity and oscillation that I have analyzed extensively in *La Voix au cinéma*.[2] We may define it as neither inside nor outside the image. It is not inside, because the image of the voice's source—the body, the mouth—is not included. Nor is it outside, since it is not clearly positioned offscreen in an imaginary "wing," like a master of ceremonies or a witness, and it is implicated in the action, constantly about to be part of it. This is why voices of clearly detached narrators are not acousmêtres. Why invent such a barbarous term? Because I wish not to be limited to terms for voices or sounds but rather to explore an entire category of *characters* specific to the sound film, whose wholly specific presence is based on their characters' very absence from the core of the image.

We can describe as acousmêtres many of the mysterious and talkative characters hidden behind curtains, in rooms or hideouts, which the sound film has given us: the master criminal of Lang's *Testament of Dr. Mabuse*, the mother in Hitchcock's *Psycho*, and the fake Wizard of Oz in the MGM film by that name; and innumerable voice-characters: robots, computers (Kubrick's *2001, A Space Odyssey*), ghosts (Ophuls's *Tendre ennemie*), certain voices of narrators that have mysterious properties (Mankiewicz's *Letter to Three Wives*, Welles's *Magnificent Ambersons*, Sternberg's *Anatahan*, the beginning of Preminger's *Laura*, Bertolucci's *Tragedy of a Ridiculous Man*, but also Raul Ruiz's *The One-Eyed Man* or the beggar woman in Marguerite Duras's *India Song*.

Fiction films tend to grant three powers and one gift to the acousmêtre, to the voice that speaks over the image but is also forever on the verge of appearing in it. First, the acousmêtre has the power of *seeing all*; second, the power of *omniscience*; and third, the *omnipotence* to act on the situation. Let us add that in many cases there is also a gift of *ubiquity*—the acousmêtre seems to be able to be anywhere he or she wishes. These powers, however, often have limits we do not know about, and are thereby all the more disconcerting.

First, this voice that speaks over the images can see everything therein. This power arises from the notion that in a sense the acousmêtre is the very voice of what is called *primary identification* with the camera. The power manifests itself vividly in stories of the harassing phone caller whose "voice" sees everything—for example, John Carpenter's *Murder on the 43rd Floor*. The second power, omniscience, of course derives from the first. As for the third, this is precisely the power of *textual speech* (see chapter 9), intimately connected to the idea of magic, when the words one utters have the power to become things.

I shall call *paradoxical acousmêtres* those deprived of some powers that are usually accorded to the acousmêtre; their lack is the very thing that makes them special. There are such "partial" acousmêtres in *India Song* and *Anatahan*. Also in two of Terence Malick's films, *Badlands* and *Days of Heaven*, the female narrators do not see or understand everything in the images over which they are speaking.

An inherent quality of the acousmêtre is that it can be instantly dispossessed of its mysterious powers (seeing all, omniscience, omnipotence, ubiquity) when it is *de-acousmatized*, when the film reveals the face that is the source of the voice. At this point, through synchronism, the voice finds itself attributed to and confined to a body. Why is the sight of the face necessary to de-acousmatization? For one thing, because the face represents the individual in her singularity. For another, the sight of the speaking face attests through the synchrony of audition/vision that the voice really belongs to that character, and thus is able to capture, domesticate, and "embody" her (and humanize her as well).

De-acousmatization consists of an unveiling process that is unfailingly dramatic. Its most typical form occurs in detective and mystery films, when the "big boss" who pulls all the strings—a character we haven't seen but only heard, and perhaps glimpsed the shoes of—is finally revealed. This unmasking occurs, for example, in Aldrich's *Kiss Me Deadly* and Terence Young's *Dr. No.*

Pascal Bonitzer has noted that the de-acousmatization of a character generally goes hand in hand with his descent into a human, ordinary, and vulnerable fate. As long as we can't see him we attribute all-seeing power to the voice; but once inscribed in the visual field he loses his aura. De-acousmatization can also be called embodiment: a sort of enclosing of the voice in the circumscribed limits of a body—which tames the voice and drains it of its power.

The acousmêtre's person seems to inhabit the image, by its nature blurring the boundaries between onscreen and offscreen. But it can maintain its particular status only as long as this onscreen-offscreen distinction prevails in a meaningful way. The acousmêtre's existence by no means constitutes a refutation of the onscreen-offscreen duality; quite to the contrary, it draws its very force from the opposition and from the way it transgresses it.

Logically enough, recent modifications in cinematic space— transformed as it has been by multitrack sound and a wrap-around "superfield," which problematize older and simpler notions of onscreen and offscreen—are putting the acousmêtre on shakier ground. And in fact, the recent cinema has fewer of them.[3]

Suspension

In Imamura's *Ballad of Narayama* the son, who is carrying his mother to the mountains so she can die according to proper custom, has paused along his way, and he stands drinking water at a spring coming out of a rock. He looks around and suddenly freezes: his mother seems to have vanished into thin air. At this moment the spring we continue to see flowing nearby abruptly ceases making any sound: auditively, it has dried up. This is an example of suspension.

Suspension is specific to the sound film, and one could say it represents an extreme case of null extension. Suspension occurs when a sound naturally expected from a situation (which we usually hear at first) becomes suppressed, either insidiously or suddenly. This creates an impression of emptiness or mystery, most often without the spectator knowing it; the spectator feels its effect but does not consciously pinpoint its origin.

Now and then, as in the dream of the snowstorm in Kurosawa's *Dreams*, suspension may be more overt. Over the closeup of an exhausted hiker who has lain down in the snow, the howling of the wind disappears but snowflakes continue to blow about silently in the image. We see a woman's long black hair twisted about by the wind in a tempest that makes no sound, and all we hear now is a supernaturally beautiful voice singing.

An effect of *phantom sound* is then created: our perception becomes filled with an overall massive sound, mentally associated with all the micromovements in the image. The pullulating and vibrating surface that we see produces something like a noise-of-the-image. We perceive large currents or waves in the swirling of the snowflakes on the screen surface. The fadeout of sound from the tempest has led us to invest the image differently. When there was sound it told us of the storm. When the sound is removed our beholding of the image is more interrogative, as it is for silent cinema. We explore its spatial dimension more easily and spontaneously; we tend to look more actively to the image to tell us what is going on.

Kurosawa has a fondness for suspensions; he also used them in *Ran*—for example, in the scene in Hell, a terrifying, mute battle, accompanied only by composer Takemitsu's music.

Often just one audio element of the soundscape is "suspended," with the result of heightening one moment of the scene, giving it a striking, disquieting or magical impact: for example, when crickets suddenly stop chirping. Generally suspension relies on the film's characters not noticing nor alluding to it. (An altogether different effect arises when it is the plot situation itself that logically leads to silence, for example a noisy crowd that calms down.)

At the end of Fellini's *Nights of Cabiria*, the prostitute with a heart of gold played by Giulietta Masina believes she has finally found her Prince Charming in a traveling salesman (François Périer). They go for a romantic walk together at sunset in the woods next to a cliff. The spectator experiences a vague anxiety about what is going to happen: we will discover that all the man wanted was Cabiria's money and that he was planning to push her over the cliff to her death. Where did our premonitory anxiety come from? From the fact that over this magical landscape not a single birdsong is heard.

Here, suspension functions according to such a common audiovisual convention (sun-dappled woods = birdsongs) that to perturb it is all that's needed to generate strangeness (Fellini, unlike Kurosawa, has not begun the scene with tweeting). Chabrol also used this device in his fantasy-film *Alice ou la dernière fugue*. The lovely woodland landscape through which Sylvia Krystel moves as a traveler between life and death is often emptied, sucked from within by the suspensive silence that reigns there, and by the absence of natural murmurings of birds or wind—an absence that only exists as such because we hear over these images the heroine's voice and footsteps.

In *Rear Window* the scene mentioned earlier is based as much on an effect of suspension as on telescoped extension: not only do the killer's steps resonate differently in the silence that has come over the sequence but the whole city and the courtyard seem to be holding their breath as well.

"Visualists" of the Ear, "Auditives" of the Eye

Sound and image are not to be confused with the ear and the eye. We find proof of this in filmmakers who infuse their images with what may be called the auditive impulse. What does this mean? Cinema can give us much more than Rimbaudian correspondences ("Black A, white E, red I"); it can create a veritable intersensory reciprocity. Into the image of a film you can inject a sense of the auditory, as Orson Welles or Ridley Scott have. And you can infuse the soundtrack with visuality, as Godard has. What does it mean to be a sound-thinker, if it's not a matter of sensations addressed literally to the ear?

From Scott's very first film, *The Duellists*, one can note the English director's passion for making light flutter, vibrate, murmur, twinkle on all kinds of occasions. In *Legend* we see spots of moving and glistening light in undergrowth where leaves are blowing in the wind. *Blade Runner* has the headlights of flying vehicles, which ceaselessly sweep through the interior of an apartment of the future. In the New York of *Someone To Watch Over Me* steam springing from an infernal underground perpetually under pressure forms a halo of shifting whiteness behind the characters. Then there is the nightclub's strobe-light show hacking the scene into ultrarapid microperceptions. We get the feeling that this visual volubility, this luminous patterning is a transposition of sonic velocity into the order of the visible.

I have said elsewhere that the ear's temporal resolving power is incomparably finer than that of the eye; and film demonstrates this especially clearly in action scenes. While the lazy sphere thinks it sees continuity at twenty-four images per second, the ear demands a much higher rate of sampling. And the eye is soon outdone when the image shows it a very brief motion; as if dazed, the eye is content to notice merely that something is moving, without being able to analyze the phenomenon. In this same time the ear is able to recognize and to etch clearly onto the perceptual screen a complex series of auditory trajectories or verbal phonemes.

Conversely, some kinds of rapid phenomena in images appear to be addressed to, and registered by, the *ear that is in the eye*, in order to be converted into auditory impressions in memory. Ridley Scott takes pleasure in combining large and resonant sound expanses with a teeming visual texture. The former can very easily turn into visual memories (of space), while the latter will leave the impression of something heard.

We can think also of that great auditively oriented director Welles, who cultivated rapid editing and dialogue, and whose films leave the impression in the spectator's memory of a superabundance of sound effects. Curiously, careful videotape screenings reveal that the soundtracks are not as profuse as they seem. *Citizen Kane* and *Touch of Evil* certainly do sometimes present localized contrasts of audio planes (foreground-background) and some echo effects on the voices, but these do not suffice to explain the intensely auricular, symphonic memory that the whole of Welles's work leaves us with. This quality suggests rather a *conversion* in memory: impressions of speed are produced most obviously by the flow of speech and fast overlapping of voices, but also—above all—by the visual rhythm.

Is there such a thing as "visualists of the ear," the opposite of "auditives of the eye"? Perhaps Godard, in that he loves to edit sounds as shots are edited (with cuts), and in that he loves to make these voices and noises resonate in a reverberant and tangible space, such that we sense a real interior with walls: the hospital room in *First Name Carmen*, the café in *Masculine-Feminine*, the classrooms in *Band of Outsiders* and *La Chinoise*. Now these acoustical effects of reverberant and prolongued sounds often leave us a memory that is more visual than auditory. For example, I have always remembered Bresson's film *A Man Escaped*, which I saw very young, as being full of immense vistas inside prisons. It took seeing the film again many years later to realize that in the director's usual manner the frame was always rigorously restricted. A cell door, a few steps of a flight of stairs, part of a landing: these were the longest shots he allowed himself. It was admirably, obsessively executed sound—of echoing footsteps, guards' repeated whistles and shouts—that engraved these Piranesian images into my childhood memory.

If we extend this idea far enough, we might conclude that everything *spatial* in a film, in terms of image as well as sound, is ultimately encoded into a so-called visual impression, and everything which is *temporal*, including elements reaching us via the eye, registers as an auditory impression. This might be an oversimplification. Nevertheless a phenomenological analysis of cinema need not fall under the hypnotic spell of technology. Materially speaking, the cinema uses auditory and visual channels, but this is not why it must thereby be described as a simple sum of "soundtrack" plus "image track." Rhythm, for example, is an element of film vocabulary that is neither one nor the other, neither specifically auditory nor visual.

In other words, when a rhythmic phenomenon reaches us via a given sensory path—this path, eye or ear, is perhaps nothing more than the channel through which *rhythm* reaches us. Once it has entered the ear or eye, the phenomenon strikes us in some region of the brain connected to the motor functions, and it is solely at this level that it is decoded as rhythm.

My basic thesis on transsensorial perception applies not only to rhythm but to perceptions of such things as texture and material as well, and surely to language (for which such a perspective is gaining wide recognition).

The eye carries information and sensations only some of which can be considered specifically and irreducibly visual (e.g., color); most others are transsensory. Likewise, the ear serves as a vehicle for information and sensations only some of which are specifically auditive (e.g., pitch and intervallic relations), the others being, as in the case of the eye, not specific to this sense. However—and I insist on this point—transsensoriality has nothing to do with what one might call intersensoriality, as in the famous "correspondences" among the senses that Baudelaire, Rimbaud, Claudel and others have celebrated. When Baudelaire evokes "parfums frais comme des chairs d'enfant, doux comme des hautbois" (perfumes fresh as baby skin, sweet as oboes), he is referring to an idea of intersensoriality: each sense exists in itself, but encounters others at points of contact.

In the transsensorial or even metasensorial model, which I am distinguishing from the Baudelarian one, there is no sensory given that is demarcated and isolated from the outset.[4] Rather, the senses are channels, highways more than territories or domains. If there exists a dimension in vision that is specifically visual, and if hearing includes dimensions that are exclusively auditive (those just mentioned), these dimensions are in a minority, particularized, even as they are central.

When kinetic sensations organized into art are transmitted through a single sensory channel, through this single channel they can convey all the other senses at once. The silent cinema on one hand and concrete music on the other clearly illustrate this idea. Silent cinema, in the absence of synch sound, sometimes expressed sounds better than could sound itself, frequently relying on a fluid and rapid montage style to do so. Concrete music, in its conscious refusal of the visual, carries with it visions that are more beautiful than images could ever be.

PART 2

· · ·

BEYOND SOUNDS AND IMAGES

SEVEN

SOUND FILM —
WORTHY OF THE NAME

. . .

SIXTY YEARS' REGRETS

Films projected in theaters have had soundtracks for sixty years now, and for sixty years this fact has influenced the cinema's internal development. But for the past sixty years as well people have continued to wonder whether the cinema did right in becoming "the talkies." One form of this tenacious prejudice is the widespread opinion that in all this time no valuable contributions (or almost none) have been made by sound. The Sleeping Beauty of talking cinema forever awaits her prince, her new Eisenstein or Griffith. Surely whoever holds such ideas runs no danger of being proven wrong. In fact, why not extend this criticism to cinema's visual dimension? For, indeed, not a whole lot has been dared in that department either, compared to what remains possible. Discussions of image and sound might thus easily remain stuck at the protest stage: since what we dream of doesn't exist, there's no use in getting interested in what does exist.

But rather than speculate in the abstract about what remains to be done, I would like to question whether we have properly assessed those changes that have occurred. I think there is a tendency to look at the sound film with our eyes staring directly backward, regretting (overtly or not) that the confounded thing didn't remain a nice little silent cinema, the way we once loved it.

Reevaluating the role of sound in film history and according it its true importance is not purely a critical or historical enterprise. The future of the cinema is at stake. It can be better and livelier if it can learn something valuable from its own past.

So far the history of film sound has almost always been told in relation to the supposed break it caused in a continuum. Everything since is related to the coming of sound. This rupture can conveniently be pinpointed historically, especially in that it happened to affect all the aspects of cinema at once: economic, technical, aesthetic, and so forth. But after the coming of sound, you'll find, if you leaf through essays on the subject, it is as if nothing ever occurred since. Historians continue to apply the same models and voice the same regrets that people expressed fifty years ago. But it seems to me that beyond the cinema's *discontinuous* history, marked by recognizable break points, which are like easily memorized dates of major battles, there lies a *continuous* history, made up of more progressive changes that are more difficult to detect. This is the history that interests me.

An Ontologically Visual Definition

Ontologically speaking, and historically too, film sound is considered as a "plus," an add-on. The underlying discourse goes like this: even though the cinema was endowed with synchronous sound after thirty years of perfectly good existence without it, whose soundtrack in recent years has become ever richer, crackling and pulsating, even now the cinema has kept its ontologically visual definition no less intact. A film without sound remains a film; a film with no image, or at least without a visual frame for projection, is not a film. Except conceptually: Walter Ruttmann's 1930 limit-case film *Weekend* is an "imageless film," according to its creator, consisting of a montage of sounds on an optical soundtrack. Played through the speakers, *Weekend* is nothing other than a radio program, or perhaps a work of concrete music. It becomes a film only with reference to a frame, even if an empty one.

The sound film, as I have said, is just this: sounds in reference to a locus of image projection, this locus being either occupied or empty. Sounds can abound and move through space, the image may remain impoverished—no matter, for quantity and proportion don't count here. The quantitative increase of sound we've seen in films in the last few years demonstrates this. Multiplex theaters equipped with Dolby sometimes reduce the screen to the size of a postage stamp, such that the sound played at powerful volume seems able to crush the screen with little effort. But the screen remains the focus of attention. The sound-camel continues to pass through the eye of the visual needle. Under the effect of this copious sound it is always the screen that radiates power and spectacle, and it is always the image, the gathering place and magnet for auditory impressions, that sound decorates with its unbridled splendor.

How can it work this way? Let us recall several facts about the cinema. The projector is located behind the spectator, the speaker in front. The speaker is not strictly the equivalent of a screen, but of a projector. Only doesn't the word *projector* have a different meaning here? For we must consider the mode of dissemination too. Light propagates (at least apparently) in a rectilinear manner, but sound spreads out like a gas. The equivalent of light *rays* is sound *waves*. The image is bounded in space, but sound is not.

Sound is mental, cannot be touched. An image can; this is what is done in religious ceremonies. You can touch the screen.

With film we can also say that the image is projected and the sound is a *projector*, in the sense that the latter projects meanings and values onto the image.

Today's multipresent sound has insidiously dispossessed the image of certain functions—for example, the function of structuring space. But although sound has modified the nature of the image, it has left untouched the image's centrality as that which focuses the attention. Sound's "quantitative" evolution—in quantity of amplification, information, and number of simultaneous tracks—has not shaken the image from its pedestal. Sound still has the role of showing us what it wants us to see in the image.

Nonetheless, Dolby multitrack sound, increasingly prominent since the mid-seventies, has certainly had both direct and indirect effects. To begin with, there is the new territory noises have conquered.

MULTITRACK SOUND, DIRECT AND INDIRECT EFFECTS

Revalorizing Noise

For a long time natural sound or noises were the forgotten elements, the "repressed" part of film not just in practice but also in analysis. There are a thousand studies of music (by far the easiest subject, since culturally the best understood), and numerous essays on the text of dialogues, and finally some work on the voice (a new topic that does not fail to fascinate its researchers). But noises, those humble footsoldiers, have remained the outcasts of theory, having been assigned a purely utilitarian and figurative value and consequently neglected.

For much traditional cinema this neglect is proportional to the scanty presence of noises in the films themselves. We all carry a few film sounds in our memory—the train whistle, gunshots, galloping horses in westerns and the tapping of typewriters in police station scenes—but we forget that they are heard only occasionally, and are always extremely stereotyped. In fact, in a classical film, between the music and the omnipresent dialogue, there's hardly room for anything else. Take an American film noir or a Carné-Prévert from the forties: what do the noises come down to? A few series of discreet footsteps, several clinking glasses, a dozen gunshots. And with sound quality so acoustically impoverished, so abstract, that they all seem to be cut out of the same gray, impersonal cloth. The exceptions cited in classical cinema are always the same ones, so rare, that they only prove the rule: Tati, Bresson and two or three others. That's it.

Both technical and cultural explanations for this situation suggest themselves. Technical: from the beginning the art of sound recording focused principally on the voice (spoken and sung) and on music. Much less attention was paid to noises, which presented special problems for recording; in the old films noises didn't sound good and they often interfered with the comprehension of dialogue. So filmmakers preferred to get rid of them and replace them with stylized sound effects. Cultural reasons: noise is an element of the sensory world that is totally devalued on the aesthetic level. Even cultivated people today respond with resistance and sarcasm to the notion that music can be made out of it.

When sound was just coming to film, however, there was no shortage of courageous experiments in admitting noise into the audiovisual symphony. I say courageous, because we must remember that the technical conditions of the era were hardly amenable to a satisfying or lifelike rendition of these phenomena. We find some examples with the Soviets (Vertov and Pudovkin) and the French, especially Renoir and Duvivier, who took pains to render, behind dialogue, the sonic substance of city life. The Germans were pioneers of recording and among the greatest technicians of sound. To them we owe such attempts as the astonishing *Abschied* (1930); Robert Siodmak's entire film uses for its set the interior of an apartment, and it makes extensive use of household and neighborhood sounds. These scattered experiments in the earliest sound years took advantage of the temporary banishment of music (which had issued from below the screen in the silents); they called on music only if the action justified it as diegetic. The sparsity of music made room for noises on what was a very narrow strip for optical sound.

What happened next? Pit music, which comments on the action from the privileged place of the imaginary orchestra pit, returned with a vengeance within three or four years, unseating noises in the process. The mid-thirties witnessed a tidal wave of films sporting obtrusive musical accompaniments. Sandwiched between equally prolix doses of dialogue and music, noises then became unobtrusive and timid, tending much more toward stylized and coded sound effects than a really fleshed-out rendering of life. Bear in mind that composers considered it the mission of the musical score to reconstruct the aural universe, and to tell in its own way the story of the raging storm, the meandering stream, or the hubbub of city life by resorting to an entire arsenal of familiar orchestral devices developed over the past century and a half. For illustration we need only consider Renoir's *A Day in the Coun-*

try, an open-air film par excellence. Practically the only natural sounds we hear are those expressed in a stylized way in Kosma's orchestral score, which was composed ten years after the filming, at the time of the editing and postsynching of the film.

Not until the arrival of Dolby sound did films receive a wide sound strip and a substantial number of tracks, permitting one to hear well-defined noises simultaneous with dialogue. Only then could noises have a living corporeal identity rather than merely exist as stereotypes.

Of course not all films have used this technical capability to its best advantage. The greatest sonic inventiveness has often gone into genre films—science fiction, fantasy, action and adventure films. Most of the others, including "auteur" films, have not yet given noises the status of an integral cinematic element with the recognition that above and beyond their directly figurative function they might have the same expressive capacity as lighting, framing, and acting. And let us not blame it on budgets. Sounds cost the least of anything in the production of a film.

Gains in Definition

Basing their opinion on the fact that since the late twenties sound has in most cases occupied one channel that has remained basically the same (the optical soundtrack), people often pretend to believe that nothing further developed until Dolby. In reality, all you need to do is listen to a film from the early thirties and compare it with the sound of a film of the forties, and then with a fifties film, to see that even before the widespread adoption of noise-reduction technology, significant evolution occurred in the technical area of sound definition. Whether it led to "better" sound is not so much the question; the task is first to acknowledge the changes.

If by comparison we turn to the example of the image, everyone will agree that in the sixties and seventies black and white was progressively replaced by color. This led in turn to a new status for black and white: no longer the norm, it became something unusual, an aesthetic option. For sound, parallel technical developments occurred that were just as decisive although much more gradual. If for the visual side there had been a history of almost imperceptible stages from an image consisting of absolute contrasting black and white to an image having all gradations of color and light at its disposal, this would provide a fair analogy to what has happened on the sound side.

So at the beginning of sound the frequency range was still rather limited. This meant, first, that sounds could not be mixed together too much, for fear of losing their intelligibility; second, when the soundtrack did require superimposed sounds, one sound had to be featured clearly above the others. The audio element that had primacy in the emerging talking film was not music (already present in the silent film) or noises but speech, which is the most coded element of all. Neither was there any question of designing soundtracks of any sensory complexity. The point was to give viewers something clear and distinct. Noises and music, for their part, needed to be as stereotyped as possible in order to be immediately recognizable. As the film's sound strip very gradually became wider, and as new technologies of sound mixing were developed, it became easier to produce sounds that were well-defined and individuated in the mix. The means became available to produce sounds other than conventionally coded ones, sounds that could have their own materiality and density, presence and sensuality.

The fact that this became possible certainly does not mean that everyone instantly made use of it. In fact, most filmmakers continued to rely on the same dry and impersonal noises as before.

But even so, little by little, they began to create ambient sound behind voices and beyond the musical accompaniment, which gave life to narrative space. Little by little, sound acquired a richness of detail, especially in the higher frequencies, which resulted in changing, by impregnation, the nature of the image itself.

Sound Infuses the Image

It can be said that sound's greatest influence on film is manifested at the heart of the image itself. The clearer treble you hear, the faster your perception of sound and the keener your sensation of presentness. The better-defined film sound became in the high frequency range, the more it induced a rapid perception of what was onscreen (for vision relies heavily on hearing). This evolution consequently favored a cinematic rhythm composed of multiple fleeting sensations, of collisions and spasmodic events, instead of a continuous and homogenous flow of events. Therefore we owe the hypertense rhythm and speed of much current cinema to the influence of sound that, we daresay, has seeped its way into the heart of modern-day film construction.

Further, the standardization of Dolby has introduced a sudden leap in an older and more gradual process that paved the way for it. There is perhaps as much difference between the sound of a Renoir of the early thirties and that of a fifties Bresson film as there is between the fifties Bresson and a Scorsese in eighties Dolby, whose sound vibrates, gushes, trembles, and cracks (think of the crackling of flashbulbs in *Raging Bull* and clicking of billiard balls in *The Color of Money*.)

Be that as it may, the fact remains that Dolby stereo has changed the balance of sounds, particularly by taking a great leap forward in the reproduction of noises. It has created sonic raw materials that are well defined, personalized, and no longer conventional *signs* of sound effects; and it has led to the creation of a sort of superfield, a general spatial continuum or tableau. Which changes the perception of space and thereby the rules of scene construction.

Superfield

I call *superfield* the space created, in multitrack films, by ambient natural sounds, city noises, music, and all sorts of rustlings that surround the visual space and that can issue from loudspeakers outside the physical boundaries of the screen.[1] By virtue of its acoustical precision and relative stability this ensemble of sounds has taken on a kind of quasi-autonomous existence with relation to the visual field, in that it does not depend moment by moment on what we see onscreen. But structurally speaking the sounds of the superfield also do not acquire any real autonomy, with salient relations of the sounds among themselves, which would earn the name of a true *soundtrack* (see chapter 3). What the superfield of multitrack cinema has done is progressively modify the structure of editing and scene construction.

Scene construction has for a long time been based on a dramaturgy of the establishing shot. By this I mean that in editing, the shot showing the whole setting was a strategic element of great dramatic and visual importance, since whether it was placed at the beginning, middle, or end of a given scene, it forcefully conveyed (established or reestablished) the ambient space, and at the same time re-presented the characters in the frame, striking a particular resonance at the moment it intervened.

The superfield logically had the effect of undermining the narrative importance of the long shot. This is because in a more concrete and tangible manner than in traditional monaural films the superfield provides a continuous and constant consciousness of all the space surrounding the dramatic action.

Through a spontaneous process of differentiation and complementarity favored by this superfield, we have seen the establishing shot give way to the multiplication of closeup shots of parts and fragments of dramatic space such that the image now plays a sort of solo part, seemingly in dialogue with the sonic orchestra in the audiovisual concerto.[2] The vaster the sound, the more intimate the shots can be (as in Roland Joffe's *Mission*, Milos Forman's *Hair*, and Ridley Scott's *Blade Runner*).

We must also not forget that the definitive adoption of multitrack sound occurred in the context of musical films like Michael Wadleigh's *Woodstock* or Ken Russell's *Tommy*. These rock movies were made with the intent to revitalize filmgoing by instituting a sort of participation, a communication between the audience shown in the film and the audience in the movie theater. The space of the film, no longer confined to the screen, in a way became the entire auditorium, via the loudspeakers that broadcast crowd noises as well as everything else. In relation to this global sound the image tended to become a sort of reporting-at-a-distance—a transmission by the intermediary of the camera—of things normally situated outside the range of our own vision. The image showed its voyeuristic side, acting as a pair of binoculars—in the same way that cameras allow you to see, when you're at a live rock concert, details, projected on a giant screen, otherwise inaccessible to fans in the back rows.

When multitrack sound extended into nonmusical films, and eventually into smaller dramas with no trace of grand spectacle, filmmakers retained this principle of the "surveillance-camera image." This development obviously might shock those who uphold traditional principles of scene construction, who point an accusing finger at what they call a music video style. The music video style, with its collision editing, is certainly a new development in the linear and rhythmic dimensions of the image, possibly to the detriment of the spatial dimension. The temporal enrichment of the image, which is becoming more fluid, filled with movement, and bubbling with details, has the image's spatial impoverishment as its inevitable correlate, bringing us back at the same time to the end of the silent cinema.

Toward a Sensory Cinema

Cinema is not solely a show of sounds and images; it also generates rhythmic, dynamic, temporal, tactile, and kinetic sensations that make use of both the auditory and visual channels. And as each technical revolution brings a sensory surge to cinema it revitalizes the sensations of matter, speed, movement, and space. At such historical junctures these sensations are perceived for themselves, not merely as coded elements in a language, a discourse, a narration.

Toward the end of the twenties most of the prestigious filmmakers like Eisenstein, Epstein, and Murnau were interested in sensations; having a physical and sensory approach to film, they were partial to technical experimentation. Very few of their counterparts today are innovators ready to meet challenges of new technical possibilities, especially concerning Dolby sound. A symptom, perhaps, of a new stage in the eternal "crisis" of the cinema.

Frankly, many European directors have simply ignored the amazing mutation brought on by the standardization of Dolby. Fellini, for example, makes use of Dolby in *Interview* in order to fashion a soundtrack exactly like the ones he made before. In Kubrick's latest films there is no particularly imaginative use of Dolby either. With *Wings of Desire*, Wenders puts Dolby to a kind of radiophonic use, in the great German *Hörspiel* tradition.[3] As for Godard, for whom expectations were high, he has not fundamentally revitalized his approach to sound in his two films with Dolby. Neither in *Detective* nor *Signe ta droite* does he offer anything original in lapping and joining of sounds, by comparison to what he already achieved in monaural films; in addition, for *Nouvelle Vague* he has returned to his usual monophonic technique.

We could continue down the list and note that from the oldest (Bresson) to the youngest (Carax), there seems to be a contest of who can show the least enthusiasm for the new sound resources: just about everyone either neglects them or uses them without inventing anything new. To end on a positive note we should point out Kurosawa's purity and sure hand in mastering Dolby in his *Dreams*. But there are many other directors not necessarily classified as great auteurs and many films not generally revered as great works that are developing these resources in new ways. Some recent examples: the films of David Lynch, of course, but also Coppola's *One From the Heart*, William Friedkin's *Cruising*, and Terence Malick's *Days of Heaven*.

Just what does Dolby stereo offer to a director? Nothing less than the equivalent of an eight-octave grand piano, when what she or he had before was an upright spanning only five octaves, less powerful and less capable of nuance. In short, Dolby offers a gain in resources on the level of sound space and sound dynamics that, of course, no one is obliged to use all the time but that is nevertheless available.

Let us recall that Beethoven wrote his piano sonatas for a smaller instrument than the piano of today: where he reached the limits of his keyboard, we have another two or three octaves. In this sense it is perhaps more correct to play Beethoven on the piano of his era. But there would be something absurd in seeing today's composers writing pieces for modern pianos with the same limitations as those that constrained the author of the Pathé-tique. We'd call that working with blinders; and this is precisely what many filmmakers are doing these days, irrespective of any issues of finances.

For writing big does not necessarily mean filling up the whole available space. It means that even when you write only one single note or melodic line, the empty space around the note is bigger. Dolby stereo increases the possibility of emptiness in film sound at the same time that it enlarges the space that can be filled. It's this capacity for emptiness and not just fullness that offers possibilities yet to be explored. Kurosawa has magnificently exploited this dimension in *Dreams*: sometimes the sonic universe is reduced to a single point—the sound of the rain, an echo that disappears, a simple voice.

Return to Silent Film: The Sensory Continuum

In chapter 5, we compared techniques in *The Bear* and *Who Framed Roger Rabbit*. Personal preferences aside, we discovered a certain convergence between the two films: the American one, horizontal, depends on speed, while the French one, vertical, rather works toward a certain density of reality. But don't both films share the impulse to bring to a wide family audience an attempt to render sensations, this being a preoccupation formerly reserved to a more limited audience? I'm speaking of the sci-fi and horror film (Sam Raimi, Cronenberg, Phil Kauff-mann's *Invasion of the Body Snatchers*) that used to be the privileged proving ground for such sensory experiments. This pursuit of sensations (of weight, speed, resistance, matter and texture) may well be one of the most novel and strongest aspects of current cinema. To the detriment, as some object, of delicacy of feeling, intelligence of screenwriting, or narrative rigor? Probably. But didn't the much-admired films of the old days, for their part, achieve their emotional force and dramatic purity at the expense of yet something else—of "sensation" for example, when in reproducing noises they gave us an inferior and stereotyped sensuality?

Recent American productions like John McTiernan's *Die Hard*, Steven Spielberg's *Indiana Jones and the Last Crusade*, or James Cameron's *The Abyss* have also added to this renewal of the senses in film through the playful extravagance of their plots. In these movies matter—glass, fire, metal, water, tar—resists, surges, lives, explodes in infinite variations, with an eloquence in which we can recognize the invigorating influence of sound on the overall vocabulary of modern-day film language. It is certainly looking as if an epic quality is returning to cinema, making its appearance in many films in the form of at least one fabulous sequence. Think of the Dantesque escape of the heroes, in thunder and rain, in Kontchalovsky's *Tango and Cash*, which is otherwise a pretty bad film.

The sound of noises, for a long time relegated to the background like a troublesome relative in the attic, has therefore benefited from the recent improvements in definition brought by Dolby. Noises are reintroducing an acute feeling of the materiality of things and beings, and they herald a sensory cinema that rejoins a basic tendency of . . . the silent cinema.

The paradox is only apparent. With the new place that noises occupy, speech is no longer central to films. Speech tends to be reinscribed in a global sensory continuum that envelops it, and that occupies both kinds of space, auditory and visual. This represents a turnaround from sixty years ago: the acoustical poverty of the soundtrack during the earliest stage of sound film led to the privileging of precoded sound elements, that is, language and music—at the expense of the sounds that were pure indices of reality and materiality, that is, noises.

The cinema has been the talking film for a long time. But only for a short while has it been worthy of the name it was given, a bit hurriedly: sound film.

EIGHT

TELEVISION, VIDEO ART, MUSIC VIDEO

. . .

TELEVISION'S OPTIONAL IMAGE

As we have seen, the image defines the cinema ontologically. Now, the difference between cinema and television lies not so much in the visual specificity of their images, as in the different roles of sound in each. In *La Toile trouée* I wrote (with no pejorative intention) that television is illustrated radio.[1] The point here is that sound, mainly the sound of speech, is always foremost in television. Never offscreen, sound is always *there*, in its place, and does not need the image to be identified. To illustrate this distinction, let us look at two works by Marguerite Duras, both shot in 16 millimeter and both presented as "films." One of them, *India*

Song, appears to me to be typically cinematic, and the other, *Le Camion*, televisual.

Anyone who has seen *India Song* knows that not a single synchronous sound issues from the image. But, from the gossipy voices of the ambassador's reception to the beautiful melodies of Carlos d'Alessio, not to mention the dialogues of the offscreen protagonists, the vice-consul's shout, the stirrings of exotic birdlife, and the exclamations of the beggar woman of Savan, all the sounds of the film congregate around the image they do not inhabit, like flies on a window pane. This is definitely cinema.

Le Camion, made two years later, also dissociates sound and image, but in a very different way. When author Duras narrates to Gérard Depardieu a film that "would be" *Le Camion*, we actually see both of them together in a sitting room. From time to time over the voice of Duras's narration there appear shots of the famous truck crossing the French countryside. Despite the fact that the image is "outside" the narration (we never see the truck's occupants), it is nothing more than an *extra image*. That is, this image of the truck is treated televisually rather than cinematically; it's similar in nature to images that might be used in TV news to illustrate or rather decorate, with the sight of a particular truck, the verbal description of some corporate problem of trucking companies.

Another typical characteristic of television is having offscreen voices *speak among themselves* by short-circuiting the visual. This occurs rarely in films, even Godard's, for in the cinema everything passes through an image or rather through a place of images. An exception is the phenomenon of gossiping voices or group commentary. Think of the voices of the classical chorus, those of the village, of the community—the voices at the beginning of Welles's *The Magnificent Ambersons*, in Duras's *India Song*, in Paradjanov's *Shadows of Forgotten Ancestors*—which talk among themselves but always about something in the image. In television there is hardly anything more common than conversations among people that do not necessarily refer to what is on screen at the time. In *Le Camion*, despite Depardieu's muteness, everything is based on the principle of a conversation that the image seems merely to illustrate or decorate. The properly televisual is the image as something extra.

ACOUSTIC SPORTS

Of all sports on television tennis is the acoustic sport par excellence. It is the only one where the commentators agree to curb their prattling so as to let us hear ten, twenty, sometimes thirty seconds of volleys without a peep out of them.

You could not follow along with your ears if you were watching soccer or a highjump competition. In boxing the hooks and uppercuts certainly do not make the noise that conventional sound effects lead us to expect. As for ping-pong, the pace of its back-and-forth hitting is too fast to follow easily. So in this sense tennis is unique in its genre. (We may wonder if it doesn't exercise the player's ear, too, more than any other competitive sport. Is there such a thing as a hard-of-hearing tennis player?)

Since the beginnings of television, sound recording of tennis matches and their broadcast sound quality have improved steadily in rendering details. Traditionally what was heard was brief thumps accompanying each hit of the ball. These constitute the sonic signature of the sport: the thump with a dry echo, by which the ear can gauge the spatial limits of the court or arena. In addition to the racquet strokes we now hear a number of small, finely delineated sound events, very well reproduced on the televised soundtrack: subtle hisses and squeaks created by the opponents' legs and feet moving across the court; panting, breathing, and sometimes grunts or shouts when the players are fatigued and playing ever harder. It's an entire acoustic narrative, but with the characteristic narrative ambiguity of the universe of sounds; we hear precisely what is happening, yet we don't *know* what is happening. There is not a different impact sound for each racquet or each player. Although the quality and, in any case, the force of the stroke can sometimes be identified, the sound does not tell us who struck the ball and where it's going.

It remains that in the game of tennis every meaningful moment is punctuated by a specific sound and each volley is an acoustic drama organized around an auditory accident: the absence of the thump signifying the ball hit and returned (either player A has sent it into the net or player B has missed it). But this sonic void, this musical rest, this *missed point of synchronization* in the alternating play of the athletes becomes immediately compensated by the nuanced waves of the voices of the crowd, their constant and unpredictable peripeteias: applause, disappointed "ooohhs . . . ," whistling. In reacting to the absence of a sound, the audience plays its own sonic and rhythmical part in the spectacle.

In a sports broadcast, of tennis matches especially, acoustic space is uncoupled from visual space. What we hear is at a stable level, always in aural long shot—even though it actually results from the sum total of points of audition of different mikes placed at stategic points on the court. On the other hand, the *image* selected by the editing crew alternates distanced perspectives (high-angle views of the whole arena) with close views (faces or feet of the players, via telephoto lenses). This differential treatment, especially in moments when one of the players is grumbling or ranting and raving, produces a type of sound-image relation that is common to televised sports broadcasts yet completely unknown to the cinema: faces of men or women in closeup, via telephoto lenses, superimposed on their faraway and indistinct voices. In short, it gives us a symmetrical "close-far" in contrast to the "far-close" more characteristic of fiction films, where the long shot of a character can be accompanied by his or her voice heard up close.

The telespectator's aural connection with the microevents of a tennis match is always subject to interruption. All it takes is a volley ending and a point being declared and the audience making a collective response for the sounds made by the players to disappear, as if their microphones suddenly shut off. Then they move, silent silhouettes, on ground that does not crunch or squeak under their feet, and the radiophonic voice commenting on them regains the upper hand.

If, finally, during the television broadcast moments of aural poetry still manage to materialize in the silences between the anchors' comments, it is a stroke of good fortune. For example, when you hear the hum of an airplane that passes by overhead, demonstrating its ignorance of the sports event with a superb feline indifference. If only television would offer this "inhabited silence" more often: a little of the sonic flow of life.

VIDEO / MOUTH

What specifically marks video art, compared to film and television? This question motivates many a critical discussion these days, but to my knowledge no response has truly been formulated. Video artists themselves are in no hurry to define the specific nature of video, which of course is their right. They often work with live feeds, participating in the spectacular and performative aspects of the medium. Alternately they may produce tapes that more closely resemble films (except the circulation of these tapes is not as strongly codified as film screenings usually are). So video swings between one extreme and the other, between one kind of image that results from events in real time and another totally fixed in advance, and also between the unicity and multiplicity of screens.

Nonetheless, there are widespread preoccupations and currents in video art: for example its frequent union with dance. This connection may well be due to the dance's concern with speed of movement. For just as the dancer can arrest movement on a pose, video can play with speeds of movement and freeze the image without changing the image's nature.

One of the great differences between video and film is that film, at least in its dominant forms, rarely engages with changing speeds and stop-action. This might be for no other reason than that such devices require complicated and costly lab work—in order to produce results that can be achieved immediately in video. For another thing, freezing the film image through lab processes marks the film, transforms its substance, and results in a loss of photographic definition—in a word, leaves its trace; while in video an image that's accelerated or altered in tempo does not thereby acquire more blemishes by virtue of being copied. This identity in nature and texture between fixed image and moving image is specific to video. Finally, video is a very great resource in terms of time and money. You can shoot at great length, erase, and record over the footage as you desire, all very cheaply. These factors help to give video a characteristic volubility, in comparison to which the film image appears very cumbersome.

At the risk of oversimplifying, let us therefore say that film may have movement *in* the image, such movement is one of its defining dimensions, one that can enter into dialogue and debate with the others; while, perhaps because of its nature, the video image in itself, born from scanning, *is* pure movement: a movement that is more prone to visual verbiage, since it has no inertia to combat.

To achieve gracefulness in the cinema (think of a musical), one must conquer the heaviness of the apparatus. In video lightness is already a given, and the problem is rather to weigh things down.

But don't the rapidity and lability of the video image ultimately bring video closer to the eminently rapid element that is text?

It is therefore natural that, alongside numerous video artists whose subject is dance, there is Gary Hill, who has taken on the particular field of experience involving the confrontation of a spoken text with an image at the same pace. One of his works, *Incidences of Catastrophe* (1988), "interprets" Maurice Blanchot's text *Thomas the Obscure* in very fluid images that show the material substance of Blanchot's book itself—the pages being flipped in closeup and following the thread of the written discourse—in alternation with sights of shifting sands and ocean waves, agitated by many visual movements that have the rapidity of a text.

Listening to a text being pronounced is an activity that puts the ear and the brain to work. In film, when language is read or spoken, the image is often left high and dry, static in relation to the verbal text. It is much easier in video to go fast visually, to the point of giving what we see on the screen the look of a talking mouth: it closes and opens, puckers, bares its teeth at great speed. And all this without needing to show the image of an actual mouth.

This visual fluttering, found in music videos and in video games, thus attains the speed of the auditory and of text. It is visible stuff to listen to, to decode, like an utterance. The image loses its quality of a relatively stable surface, and what becomes significant is the changes in its tempo or appearance.

Paradoxically, this might explain why video makers often don't know what to do with sound, aside from providing a neutral background of music or a voice. For it can be argued that everything involving sound in film—the smallest vibrations, fluidity, perpetual mobility—is already located in the video image.

Other videos by Gary Hill, such as *Primarily Speaking*, confront text and image in an even more intriguing manner. While we hear a poetic reading, we see closeups of objects that resemble fragments of small animal skeletons. The camera is constantly changing focus on these objects so that the variations in focus, the modulations of sharp and blurry on various depth planes, occur at the same pace as the text being read, and they are almost synchronous with the phonemes being uttered, suggesting a deciphering, as if they partake in a code. Here the image stirs like a mouth. Can we even continue to call it an image in the usual sense?

This question of the nature of the video image brings us around to the question of the status—or rather the nonstatus—of the frame in video.

In film the frame is important, since it is nothing less than *that beyond which there is darkness*. In video the frame is a much more relative reference. This is because, for one thing, monitors always cut off an undetermined part of the image, and for another, when we look beyond the borders, there is more to see. Since we normally behold the video image in a lighted place, the image does not act as a window through which our attention is channeled.

So in film, since we're dealing with a frame that's set in stone—even if it's "transgressed" in actual viewing through masking in theater projections or cropping for video—there is a possible tension, a potential contradiction between this frame and the objects it contains. The entire art of film has been based on this very contradiction between the container (the borders of the frame, but also the temporal limits of the shot) and the content. While in video we might say that the image *is* that which it contains, that it is modeled on its content. For example, it can become a mouth that one watches as if one were deaf.

There may well be a precise relation at the core of video art between the vagueness of the frame and the indeterminate status given to sound—since in film frame and sound are strongly inter-related, particularly through the factor of offscreen space. General-ly speaking, video art does not devote much thought to the place of sound. In the cinema the place of sound is clear: sound is deter-mined in relation to a notion of the fictional space, and this space extends beyond the frame, constantly being remodeled with changes in framing. In any case, the image is the point of departure.

In commercial television the situation is equally simple, even if better hidden. Television is fundamentally a kind of radio, "illus-trated" by images. Television sound already has its established place, which is fundamental and mandatory (silent television is inconceivable, unlike cinema). But as far as video art is concerned, we do not yet know much. This also means that there is still plen-ty of room to experiment. So, back to your monitors—but don't forget the speakers.

Image-Radio

In countries where television has not yet exploded into multiple channels running twenty-four hours a day, television continues to be considered a visual medium. But in places where it has extended its programming round the clock and infiltrated the workplace as well as the home, it must inevitably assume its radiophonic nature. I am thinking in particular of program slots on MTV that offer a bloc of music videos you can follow along with as you continue working or reading, as if you were listening to a pop radio station but have the option of glancing over and looking at images too. The image here no longer touts itself as the essential ingredient; no longer stage center, it's more like an unex-pected gift.

Music videos (visuals edited together with a song) come in all shapes and sizes, budgets, and degrees of quality. They can be vital and inventive creations—in which the verve of cartoons combines with the carnal presence of real filming. The music video has invented and borrowed an entire arsenal of devices; it's a joyous rhetoric of images. And this is the paradox of the television-of-optional-images: it liberates the eye. Never is television as visual as during some moments in music videos, even when the image is conspicuously attaching itself to some music that was sufficient to itself.

Of course not everyone agrees. Cinephiles especially attack music videos as eye-assaulting; they dislike the stroboscopic effect of the rapid editing. That's because they are judging the editing according to cinematic criteria that apply to linear narrative. But the music video is altogether different, since it does not involve dramatic time. Music video editing returns repeatedly to the same motifs, typically playing on four or five basic visual themes. Rather than serving to advance action, the editing of music videos turns the prism to show its facets. The rapid succession of shots creates a sense of visual polyphony and even of simultaneity, even as we see only a single image at a time.

"A single image at a time" is indeed a fundamental visual characteristic of both film and television—unlike their soundtrack, which unproblematically mixes layers of words, noise, and music. Exceptions to this "visual monody" remain rare. Only occasionally does a film divide the screen surface in two, three, or four subscreens, or use superimposition to hold two images simultaneously on the same surface (and when this happens, at least one of them is afflicted with transparency). In television, video technique allows for subdividing the screen more easily, more quickly, and without lab work, but this resource soon runs into the problem of the reduced size of the image, ceasing to let us see much once it is subdivided. In any case, the spatial contiguity of several images arranged side by side like frames of a comic strip has nothing to do with superimposition of a musical sort. The thing that most closely resembles the polyphonic simultaneity of sound or music on the visual level is the rapid succession of single images. Upon seeing a fast montage, the spectator's memory functions like an ideal mixer—far superior to a machine—of visual impressions interlinked in time.

This is yet another way in which the music video leads us back to the silent cinema—seemingly a paradox, since we're talking about a form constructed on music. But it is precisely insofar as music does form its basis, and none of the narration is propelled by *dialogue*, that the music video's image is fully liberated from the linearity normally imposed by sound.

Of course, the main reason music videos can function at all is because of the elementary relation between soundtrack and visual track; the two are not wholly independent from each other. But this relation is often limited to points of synchronization, where the image matches the production of sound in some way. The rest of the time each goes its separate way.

Since they are not intellectualized in their production process, music videos don't bother to be concerned about the way they combine devices that might be opposed in the abstract. Thus in the same video we might note extremely precise and pronounced synch points and, at other moments, a widespread nonsynchronizing, a total freedom of the image's behavior in relation to the sound.

There is also the particularly rich case of rap videos by some black groups—videos of speech, where certain words in the spoken text are repeated in written form. Here the word, which is in any case at the heart of the "audiologovisual," acquires an original form of existence that is not solely limited to the sound or to the image.

In the very beginnings of the silent cinema people sometimes spoke "live" to provide commentary on the images being shown.

Then, in the classical silent film era, words no longer existed except in written form, as intertitles. In the talking film it has become rare, on the other hand, to see words inscribed in the image; and even with Godard the word written on the screen has no function that ties it to the narration itself in the general sense of the term.

But in the rap video the word written electronically onto the image, or represented as in a comics balloon, is also the word that we can hear. It wanders freely, alive, between the written and the oral, abolishing the rigid barriers of the audiologovisual, showing yet another aspect of the vitality of the very current genre of the music video.

NINE

TOWARD AN
AUDIOLOGOVISUAL
POETICS

. . .

The world is in motion and in chiaroscuro. We can see only one side of things, only halfway, always changing. Their outline dissolves into shadow, reemerges in movement, then disappears in darkness or a surfeit of light. Our attention, too, is in chiaroscuro. It flits from one object to another, grasping a succession of details and then the whole. The cinema seems to have been invented to represent all of this. It shows us bodies in shadow and light; it abandons an object only to find it again, and isolates it with a dolly-in or resituates it in a dolly-out.

There is only one element that the cinema has not been able to treat this way, one element that remains constrained to perpetual clarity and stability, and that is dialogue. We seem to have to understand each and every word, from beginning to end, and not one word had better be skipped. Why? What would it matter if we lost three words of what the hero says? Yet this has remained almost taboo in films. We are only beginning to learn how; for, as we shall see, in sound film there is a lot riding on these three lost words.

Before the sound film, the silent film—in spite of its name— was by no means without language. Language was doubly present: explicitly, in the text of intertitles, and implicitly, in the very way the images were conceived, filmed, and edited to constitute a discourse, in which a shot or a gesture was the equivalent of a word or a syntagma. Shots or gestures said, "There is the house," or, "Pierre opens the door."

But the intertitle had an inherent limitation: it interrupted the images, it implied the conspicuous presence in the film of a foreign body, an impurity. At the same time it allowed great narrative flexibility, since title cards could be used to establish the story's setting, to sum up a part of the action, to issue a judgment about the characters, and of course, to give a free transcription of the spoken dialogues. In general the text merely summarized what was being said, it made no pretense to exhaustiveness. Dialogue could be presented in direct discourse or indirect discourse ("she explains to him that . . . "). In short, the silent film had the entire narrative arsenal of the novel at its disposal.

The sound film put an end to this, at least in its early stages, by reducing text in the film virtually to one single form: dialogues spoken in the present tense by characters. This remains the predominant mode today. The transition did not occur overnight. Over a five- or six-year period various formulas were tried before almost all films settled definitively into this paradigm of the dialogue film. But direct dialogue was not the only possible model, and I wish to explore its two exceptions.

Let me distinguish three modes of speech in film (in the case where speech is really heard, and not just suggested or hinted at). I call them *textual speech*, *theatrical speech*, and *emanation speech*.[1]

THEATRICAL SPEECH

In theatrical speech, which is the most common, the dialogue heard has a dramatic, psychological, informative, and affective function. It is perceived as dialogue issuing from characters in the action; in contrast to textual speech, it has no power over the course of the images, and, in contrast to emanation speech, it is wholly intelligible, heard clearly word for word. It is to theatrical speech that the early talking film resorted and continues to resort on a massive scale. In special cases we may hear a character's internal voice in the present tense, analogous to a theatrical aside. But even here, the text that we hear remains a concrete element of the action, with no power over the reality shown in the image.

Theatrical speech conditions not just the soundtrack but the film's mise-en-scène in the broadest sense. From screenplay to editing, by way of setting, acting, lighting, camera movements and so on, everything is in fact conceived, almost unconsciously, to make the characters' speech into the central action and at the same time to make us forget that this speech is what structures the film. This explains the paradox according to which certain films that we remember as action films, like many American productions, are in fact dialogue films nine times out of ten, but treat the dialogue as action. The most striking example is Howard Hawks's *Rio Bravo*, but also most of Hitchcock's sound films, despite his reputed contempt for words.

The formula of having characters speak while doing something, in classical cinema, serves to restructure the film through and around speech. A door closing, a gesture someone makes, a cigarette a character lights, a camera movement or a reframing, everything can become punctuation, and therefore a heightening of speech. This makes it easier to listen to dialogue and to focus attention on its content.

In films conceived on this model even the moments when characters don't speak take on meaning as interruptions in the verbal continuum. The kiss, for example, stops characters from speaking; by interrupting the confrontation or discussion or string of justifications it can break a verbal impasse. This effect is much more cinematic than theatrical or operatic.

TEXTUAL SPEECH

Textual speech—generally that of voiceover commentaries— inherits certain attributes of the intertitles of silent films, since unlike theatrical speech it acts upon the images. Textual speech has the power to make visible the images that it evokes through sound—that is, to change the setting, to call up a thing, moment, place, or characters at will.

If textual speech can control a film's narration, of course, there no longer remains an autonomous audiovisual scene, no notion whatever of spatial and temporal continuity. The images and realistic sounds are at its mercy. Sacha Guitry played the most daringly with such a case of omnipotent textual speech in *Le Roman d'un tricheur*.[2] And since textual speech does invalidate the notion of an audiovisual scene, the cinema tends to impose a strict quota on its use. This great power is generally reserved for certain privileged characters and is only granted for a limited time.

In countless films, therefore, the textual speech of a voiceover narrator engenders images with its own logic (i.e., not that of continuity editing), just long enough to establish the film's narrative framework and setting. Then it disappears, allowing us to enter the diegetic universe. We might not be reminded of the narrator's presence for the next quarter of an hour into the film, even an hour. Often the story in between has become completely autonomous from the textual speech, in creating its own dramatic time, and in showing us scenes that the voiceover narrator could not possibly have seen. The latter can actually be a protagonist, or a secondary character as witness (Truffaut's *The Woman Next Door*), or, alternatively, an external, all-seeing novelistic narrator. The third case bears obvious similarities to the position of the narrator in the traditional novel, the primary difference being that here, words become actualized.

The encounter between an all-seeing narrative textual speech and a cinematic image can be interesting even when there is "redundancy." This formula furnishes the material for numerous gags in Woody Allen's *Annie Hall*. And some of the earliest talking films, such as Fritz Lang's *M* and *The Testament of Dr Mabuse*, exhibit the temptation to play liberally with textual speech, frequently conferring it on characters in the action and thereby threatening to destroy any sense of continuity and consistency in the diegetic universe.

Textual speech is inseparable from an archaic power: the pure and original pleasure of transforming the world through language, and of ruling over one's creation by naming it. Such an intoxication has been observed in people deaf since birth, when language allows them suddenly to understand the meaning of abstraction.

Textual Speech vs. the Image

At first glance, literature seems well acquainted with the written equivalent of this approach, with its story-within-a-story constructions so common in certain narrative traditions (*The Thousand and One Nights*, Potocki's *Saragossa Manuscript*, and the English novels pastiched by Diderot in *Jacques le fataliste*). But in comparison with literature, textual speech in film is doubly powerful. Not only does it cause things to appear in the mind but also before our eyes and ears.

This power is countered by another: no sooner is something evoked visually and aurally by the word that gives birth to it than immediately we see how that which arises escapes from the abstraction of language because it's concrete, fortified with details. The image creates sensations that words could never evoke, no matter how much they tried. If for example the text-voice of the film evokes a woman by spelling her name, and if this woman is seen wearing a scarf—this scarf, not spoken by the text, is what we will see. A sort of mutual challenge arises here. The text seems to create images as it wishes, but the image retorts, "you're incapable of telling me all."

This is why, in so many occurrences of textual speech in films, the mise-en-scène takes care to give the image a stylized, artificial, and general turn (by controlling light, setting, and costumes), as if to bring the image more closely in line with the text and partially fill the gulf. This happens in Lang's *M*, where the abstract settings and the frequent absence of any concrete reference to time, place, and weather render the image more docile.

Other filmmakers, on the contrary, like to accentuate the gulf between narrative speech and image and to create contradiction, gaps, discord between the two. Not surprisingly, these include Orson Welles (*The Magnificent Ambersons*) and Michel Deville (*La Lectrice*, *Voyage en douce*), directors who are particularly interested in the question of power. Indeed, in their films the point is to determine which has the upper hand, the word or the image. Finally, there are many films that use this confrontation playfully, in the form of gags, old as the cinema itself, where the image gives the lie to the text—or rather, obeys it by making fun of it.

A Special Case: The Wandering Text

Godard's video *Letter to Freddy Buache* (1982) owes its renown no doubt to its concision and simplicity of means. Godard received a commission to celebrate the five-hundredth anniversary of the city of Lausanne. The ingredients of his piece: the author's voice addressing Freddy Buache, telling how the film should have been made (not without a hint of complaint and regret), images of Godard operating camera and sound equipment (but we don't see him speaking in synch sound), silent shots panning across Lausanne and the surrounding countryside, and a musical accompaniment for the whole thing provided by Ravel's *Bolero*.

The device of having a voice speaking over a city is not terribly original in itself. Godard's film stands apart from the usual documentary in the particular nature of the voice that dominates (or rather refuses to dominate) the image, by the particular nature of the image track, and by the distinctively "meandering" form of their relationship.

Godard's voice (we're not sure whether he is reading from written notes or completely improvising) does not pronounce a "finished" text. The voice speaks as if searching for the right words; it repeats, hesitates, fumbles, and recovers, finds a phrasing that sounds right, good enough to write ("the sky and the water," "the city is fiction" . . .). When tracking along, the camera, too, seems to be searching, stopping, starting up again, thinking, feeling its way. There is little direct synchronization of meaning between the spoken discourse and the image, only several brief encounters and some general convergences. Nevertheless, at certain moments, the affirmative tone taken by the voice finds

itself suddenly coinciding with a visual cut, as if something—
meaning, coherence—had been found.[3] These moments are like
flashpoints, points of synchronization when something "jells,"
before becoming diluted once more in the flows of words and
images.

Text as well as images refer both to the horizontal dimension
(railroad tracks, surface of the water, ground) and to the vertical
(the camera moves up and down trees and signs). Everything
plays on hesitation and the diagonals between one and the other.

The *Letter to Freddy Buache* in fact has a precursor in a work I'd
be very surprised if Godard didn't know: Guitry's *Le Roman
d'un Tricheur*. In this 1935 film, narrated throughout by Guitry's
own voice in the first person and practically devoid of synch
sound, one sequence consists of a description of the principality
of Monaco. The description is based on rhetorical oppositions
such as city/village and casino/palace. The camera emphasizes
these binarisms by dutifully flash-panning from one point to
another, expressing childish jubilation in submitting the look to
the voice. Godard constructs similar rhetorical oscillations:
up/down, sky/water, city stones/natural rock formations,
which to greater or lesser degrees are echoed in the image, in
some edits and camera movements. A major difference, however, is that while Guitry's camera moves rapidly and submits
completely to the vocal text, Godard's camera dawdles, seems
prey to the temptation to linger on things it discovers along the
way, such as the odd tree, sign, line on the ground. The camera
stumbles, and sometimes in this stumbling it seems to make little discoveries, as the Sunday walker might notice a stone, a
pebble, or the body of a dead animal. And all along, between the
meandering speech and the equally wandering image, Ravel's
music implacably pursues its course, playing the part of a
straight line of reference.

Emanation Speech

Despite its relative infrequency, textual speech has been considerably discussed and theorized, often viewed in film as an annex or outgrowth of literature. The third mode, which I call *emanation speech*, generally continues to go unnoticed, inasmuch as it is antiliterary and antitheatrical.

Emanation speech is speech which is not necessarily heard and understood fully, and in any case is not intimately tied to the heart of what might be called the narrative action. The effect of emanation speech arises from two situations. First, dialogue spoken by characters is not totally intelligible. Second, the director may direct the actors and use framing and editing in ways that run counter to the standard rules—*avoiding* emphasis on articulations of the text, the play of questions and answers, important hesitations and words. Speech then becomes a kind of emanation of the characters, an aspect of themselves, like their silhouette is—significant but not essential to the mise-en-scène and action.

Emanation speech, while the most cinematic, is thus the rarest of the three types of speech, and, for complex reasons, the sound film has made very little use of it. Still, we find it in the films of Jacques Tati and, in different ways, in Tarkovsky, Fellini, and Ophuls, as well as in smaller doses in other films.[4]

In one way, the three types of speech could be present in the silent cinema, since the characters expressed themselves abundantly, and very little of what they said was "translated." So the mise-en-scène was not forced to underline the dialogue word for word. With sound, this freedom disappeared little by little. As the cinema adopted and restructured itself around theatrical speech, it would increasingly align itself with the model of a linear verbal continuum.

Filmmakers were aware of this risk. From the very beginning of sound, many of them sought to *relativize speech*. They attempted to inscribe speech in a visual, rhythmic, gestural, and sensory totality where it would not have to be the central and determining element.

Relativizing speech might mean a number of different things. It could mean relativizing the meanings of words by countering them with a parallel or contradictory image.[5] But it might also consist of, alternately, bringing out then drowning speech in a swell of noise, music, or conversation. Or it might mean creating a proliferation of speech, offering it up to the ear in such quantity that we cannot follow any one line word for word. Technically, it could also consist of combining speech with noise, thereby removing some of its clarity, definition, and intelligibility. Let us consider several of these modes in turn.

Techniques of Relativizing Speech in the Sound Film

The question being considered here is not simple, and it has many aspects: technical, historical, aesthetic, linguistic. It has long been technically feasible to create *verbal chiaroscuro*, either through direct sound or in postsynchronization. By verbal chiaroscuro I mean a recording of human speech, in which we can understand what is said at one moment and at another understand less, or even nothing at all.

For many years it has been possible, for example during filming, to get two simultaneous recordings of the same voice, one well-defined and the other less so. Then, in mixing, you can alternate subtly and continously between one and the other as needed. But this is done quite rarely.[6] I am not suggesting that this process would be totally unproblematic technically—but preserving dialogue intelligibility throughout a film isn't either. The rarity of emanation speech is therefore more of an aesthetic and cultural problem than a technical one.

But there have been several other scattered efforts at relativization of speech, particularly during the early sound period.

Rarefaction The simplest approach involves rarefying the presence of speech. René Clair is noteworthy for doing this in his early thirties films, especially *Sous les toits de Paris*. In principle, this option allowed filmmakers to conserve many visual values of the silent cinema. But it involved two problems as well. For one thing, it obliged the filmmaker to create plot situations that would explain the absence of the voice—such as characters behind windows, distance, and crowds. For another, we experience a sense of emptiness between the few sequences with synch dialogue—or perhaps it is these sequences themselves that sound like something alien to the body of the film. Another very similar instance occurs with the dialogue scenes in one of the few modern films to have reworked Clair's approach—Stanley Kubrick's *2001, A Space Odyssey*, where speech in fact is restricted to just a few localized scenes.

Proliferation and Ad Libs The second approach uses a contrary strategy to achieve a similar effect. By accumulation, superimposition, and proliferation, words cancel one another out, or rather they nullify their influence on the film's structure. Characters may talk at the same time, quickly overlap their lines, or say "unimportant" things. In his film *La tête d'un homme* (1933), filled with various sound experiments, Julien Duvivier makes several scenes into a collective hubbub, a proliferation of speech around an event. This happens, for example, during the scene of an automobile breakdown (which the police have simulated in order to allow a suspect to escape so that they can follow him to the culprit). In the scene of the car breakdown the relativization of speech is reinforced by the disjunction between speech and the image. The image focuses on details of characters' gestures and thereby avoids showing them speaking. But when we watch the whole film we sense that these scenes are not integrated fluidly into the rest of the film, which treats dialogue in a more conventional manner.

After the early sound period this practice was retained only for specific and localized scenes, particularly meal scenes. Moments in these scenes resemble theater plays, when the stage directions call for "crowd noise" using ad-libbing. One finds such meal scenes in Renoir's *La Chienne*, Bergman's *Hour of the Wolf*, and Ridley Scott's *Alien*.

Multilingualism and Use of a Foreign Language A few films have relativized speech by using a foreign language that is not understood by most of their viewers. A related strategy is to mix several tongues, resulting in their mutual relativization.

In *Anatahan* Josef von Sternberg uses Japanese actors who speak in their own language, and who are neither subtitled nor dubbed. The voiceover narrator (Sternberg himself) summarizes the story and dialogues in English, and in this way distances us from the action. As in a silent film, we find ourselves relying on a secondary text in order to follow what the characters are saying. For *Et la lumière fut* (And then there was light, 1989) Otar Iosseliani does the same thing with African characters.

In many scenes in *Death in Venice* Visconti makes use of the story's setting (an international beach for rich foreigners) to mix languages, weaving together Hungarian, French, English, and Italian. Tati indulges in the same technique in *Playtime*, as does Fellini in several films.

Narrative Commentary Over Dialogue In some films the voiceover narrator partially covers the dialogues spoken by characters, thereby relativizing the dialogues and their content. This device occurs in Ophuls's *Le Plaisir.*

Submerged Speech Certain scenes are based on the idea of a "sound bath" that conversations alternately dive into and reemerge from. In this strategy the director uses the plot situation itself as an alibi—in a crowd scene or in a natural setting—to reveal words and then conceal them; this contributes to locating human speech in space and relativizing it. We have seen the use of this procedure in Tati's *Mr. Hulot's Holiday.* A general chattering on the soundtrack in scenes on the beach or in the hotel restaurant occasionally allows a distinct phrase or sentence to poke through and be heard.

Loss of Intelligibility Sometimes there is not only a flux and reflux of speech in the sound totality but the spectator is clearly aware of a loss of the voice's intelligibility at specific points. In his first talking film, *Blackmail*, Hitchcock attempted a famous experiment in loss of vocal intelligibility, with the idea of expressing the heroine's subjectivity. The night before, she killed a man who tried to rape her, and now she fears that her guilt will be discovered. She hears a neighbor chatting about the crime, and in the woman's stream of words we hear only the word *knife* (the murder weapon). This attempt at a *word closeup*, just as there are closeups of faces and objects, was very courageous, but it has remained an isolated case. Hitchcock himself repeated the experiment only once or twice, for example in *Rope.*

What is the problem with this method? In this scrambling of the voice that loses speech in a haze of sound with occasional moments of clarity, we hear only a technical device instead of a subjective experience. The visual equivalent of the same device—going out-of-focus to express loss of consciousness—is, on the other hand, widely accepted, having become a standard rhetorical figure of the image.

Part of the problem has to do with the particular nature of aural attention as compared to visual perception. As easy as it is to eliminate something from our field of vision, by turning our head or closing our eyes, it is quite difficult for the ear—especially in such a selective way. What we do not actively listen to our ears listen to nonetheless. They inscribe the sound onto our brain as onto magnetic tape, whether we listen to it or not, even—and especially—during sleep. Fluctuations in aural attention, therefore, are not correctly translated by varying sound clarity.

At least one director, Max Ophuls, tried to create chiaroscuro sound without resorting to extreme dramatic situations. Frequently in his films a voice's definition, and thus its intelligibility, varies from moment to moment. This variation is inextricably linked to the fact that Ophuls's characters move around a lot as they speak, and the noises they make in so doing partially drown their speech. Elsewhere Ophuls uses music, acoustical properties of the setting, and so forth, to achieve this supple fluctuation of clarity and indistinctness that for him is very closely related to the movement of life itself.

Decentering Finally, we will mention a more subtle approach to relativizing speech that, rather than drawing on acoustical qualities, makes use of the entire mise-en-scène. In *decentering* the clarity and intelligibility of the text are respected but all the filmic elements (acting and movement, framing, editing, and even screenplay) are not centered around speech and therefore do not encourage us to listen to the dialogue—so that speech seems to go one way and the rest of the film's elements go another. For example, in Fellini's or Tarkovsky's films we understand just about everything acoustically, but the editing and the acting do not emphasize the content of the lines. Scorsese gets the same effect with the voiceover of *Goodfellas*, and the impression is entirely strange.

What Godard does with the text in his films does not, in my opinion, involve what I am calling decentering. In his work, even when the text is masked by other sounds or by strong reverberation in the voices, it remains the center of attention, and a basic structuring element.

What we might call the *decentered talking film*, using emanation speech, is something else again—a polyphonic cinema. We find prefigurations and examples of it not only in the work of certain auteur directors but also in contemporary action or special-effects films. The use of different sensory effects and the presence of various sensations and rhythms in such films give us the feeling that the world is not reduced to the function of *embodying dialogue*.

ENDLESS INTEGRATION

In a certain sense this new decentered talking film is like the silent cinema, but with the addition of sound. It might well mark the third period of narrative cinema, a period of reincorporating values that speech had led the cinema to throw onto the scrap heap. Of course, this "third cinema" can only exist in the form of promises, fragments, baby steps, as parts of films that generally stick to the conventions of traditional verbocentric cinematic *écriture*. We must accept that nonhomogeneity guarantees the cinema's vitality and originality in the present era.

The history of film can thus be told as an endless movement of integrating the most disparate elements: sound and image, the sensory and the verbal. A given period might witness a successful fusion, but at the price of many simplifications and impasses, and a dictatorship of one element over the others. And there are other periods, like today, when we see new explorations and evolutions, when the cinema explodes in its disparity but creates marvelous things in the process. This happened in the fifties with American musicals. Celebrated later on through fabulous excerpted clips, the musicals in their day were only bearable for the ten or twenty minutes of greatness in each (more than enough for those who loved them). Why? Because the intervention of song and music decentered the system, creating imbalances and difficulties but also wonderful moments. The situation today is similar in many action and special-effects films.

These films foreground an incongruity at their core, arising from the copresence of new approaches with traditional editing and realist mise-en-scène in much the same way that opera, at a certain stage in its history, was obliged to accept the cohabitation of recitative and song. The journey is not yet over. The way is open to new Wagners, who will emerge in the context of auteur cinema or genre cinema and seek new solutions to the perpetual problem of integrating the real with the verbal.

Sometimes the answer may appear thanks to a good screenplay, great actors, and smart and sensitive directing. This happened with Randa Haines's *Children of a Lesser God*, which I have often mentioned in this volume. The originality of the basic plot situation—a deaf-mute woman saying things in her gestural language, which, for our convenience, her lover translates out loud—creates for the spectator of this sound film an altogether new paradigm: we *see* in the image the words we hear at the same time. Mostly, of course, we don't understand them, but, in any case, we can relate to another form of encounter (whether or not it's destined to failure) between the sensory world and the register of words.

TEN

INTRODUCTION TO AUDIOVISUAL ANALYSIS

. . .

Audiovisual analysis aims to understand the ways
in which a sequence or whole film works in its use of sound combined with its use of images. We undertake such analysis out of
curiosity, for the sake of pure knowledge, but with another goal
too, that of aesthetic refinement. For reasons we have already
examined, sound seems to remain much more difficult to categorize than images, and there remains the risk of seeing the audiovisual relationship as a repertoire of illusions, even tricks—all the
more contemptible for being so. Audiovisual analysis does not

involve clear entities or essences like the shot, but only "effects," something considerably less noble.

In the long run, it is important in our research and its applications to establish objects and categories. But first and foremost, we need to rediscover a certain freshness in how we actually apprehend films; and we'll need to discard time-worn concepts, which served mainly to *prevent* us from hearing and seeing anyway.

The kind of audiovisual analysis that I propose (and that is only briefly sketched out in this chapter) is also an exercise in humility with respect to the film, television, or video sequences we audio-view. "What do I see?" and "What do I hear?" are serious questions, and in asking them we exercise our freedom and renew our relation to the world. They also lead us into a process of stripping away old layers that guarded our own perceptions, which we've been feebly protecting as if somehow they could only survive in shameful obscurity, hidden away from others.

Audiovisual analysis must rely on words, and so we must take words seriously—whether they are words that already exist, or ones being invented or reinvented to designate objects that begin to take shape as we observe and understand. The lion's share of this work of naming remains to be done, particularly naming auditory qualities and perceptions. But even so, every language already offers a certain corpus of words that designate different types of sounds. Some of these words are quite precise and evocative. There is no reason to consider them the exclusive reserve of novelists. The terms *clink*, *screech*, and *murmur*, as opposed to less specialized words, can lend considerable precision to descriptions of sonic phenomena. Why say "a sound," when we can say "crackling" or "rumbling" or "tremolo"? Using more exact words allows us to confront and compare perceptions and to make progress in pinpointing and defining them. The simple fact of having to seek in language what you already have before your ears incites you to be more finely attuned to sounds.

We can also draw on recent work which, although often tentative and incomplete, is always interesting in its attempts to develop ways to classify sound through new descriptive criteria that lie outside the narrow field of traditional musicological studies.

METHODS OF OBSERVATION

Masking

In order to observe and analyze the sound-image structure of a film we may draw upon a procedure I call the *masking method*. Screen a given sequence several times, sometimes watching sound and image together, sometimes masking the image, sometimes cutting out the sound. This gives you the opportunity to hear the sound as it is, and not as the image transforms and disguises it; it also lets you see the image as it is, and not as sound recreates it. In order to do this, of course, you must train yourself to really see and really hear, without projecting what you already know onto these perceptions. It requires discipline as well as humility. For we have become so used to "talking about" and "writing on" things without any resistance on their part, that we are greatly vexed to see this stupid visual material and this vile sonic matter defy our lazy efforts at description, and we are tempted to give in and conclude that in the last analysis, images and especially sound are "subjective." Having reached this conclusion we can move on to serious matters like theory . . .

There is probably no ideal order in which to observe an audiovisual sequence. But I propose that discovering the sonic elements and the visual elements separately, before putting them back together again, will dispose us most favorably to keep our listening and looking fresh, open to the surprises of of audiovisual encounters. For we should keep in mind that the audiovisual contract never creates a total fusion of the elements of sound and image; it still allows the two to subsist separately while in combination. The audiovisual contract actually remains a juxtaposition at the same time as it creates a combination.

The trickiest stage of the masking procedure involves listening to the sound by itself, acousmatically. Technically, this must be done in a relatively dead sound environment that is well isolated from outside noises—conditions which must be carefully arranged. Second, participants must be willing to concentrate. We are not at all used to listening to sounds, especially nonmusical sounds, to the exclusion of anything else. It is important to plan ahead not only for a VCR and monitor but also for a small stereo system to plug into the VCR's audio output so as to have better quality and higher-volume sound capability.

Forced Marriage

One very striking experiment, which I can never recommend highly enough for studying an audiovisual sequence, is what I call *forced marriage* between sound and image. Take a sequence of a film and also gather together a selection of diverse kinds of music that will serve as accompaniment. Taking care to cut out the original sound (which your participants must not hear at first or know from prior experience), show them the sequence several times, accompanied by these various musical pieces played over the images in an aleatory manner. Success assured: in ten or so versions there will always be a few that create amazing points of synchronization and moving or comical juxtapositions, which always come as a surprise.

Changing music over the same image dramatically illustrates the phenomena of added value, synchresis, sound-image association, and so forth. By observing the kinds of music the image "resists" and the kinds of music cues it yields to, we begin to see the image in all its potential signification and expression.

Only afterward should you reveal the film's "original" sound, its noises, its words, and its music, if any. The effect at that point never fails to be staggering. Whatever it is, no one would ever have imagined it that way beforehand; we conceived of it differently, and we always discover some sound element that never would have occurred to us. For a few seconds, then, we become conscious of the fundamental strangeness of the audiovisual relationship: we become aware of the *incompatible* character of these elements called sound and image.

Standard Outline for Analysis

Dominant Tendencies and Overall Description

First, simply itemize the different audio elements present. Is there speech? music? noise? Which is dominant and foregrounded? at what points?

Characterize the general quality of the sound and particularly its *consistency*. The soundtrack's consistency is the degree of interaction of different audio elements (voices, music, noise). They may combine to form a general texture or, on the contrary, each may be heard separately, legibly. We may easily note the difference in consistency between the films of Tati, where sounds are very distinct from one another, and a Renoir film, where they are mixed together. In Tarkovsky's *Stalker* the sounds are very detached from one another: voices that sound close and distinct, sounds of drops of water, and so on. In *Alien*, on the other hand, voices are enmeshed with natural sounds within a sonic continuum of voices, music, and noise. This is appropriate for a science-fiction film full of technological devices that are constantly transmitting human voices with varying degrees of fidelity.

Consistency is a function of several factors. First, it is determined by the general balance of sound elements—speech, sound effects, music—each of which struggles to arise to intelligibility. Second, there is the degree of reverberation, which can blur the outlines of sounds and create a sort of softness linking the sounds to one another. Third, consistency depends on degrees and kinds of sound masking, which results from the coexistence of different sounds in the same frequency registers.

Spotting Important Points of Synchronization

Locate the key points of synchronization, the primary synch points that are crucial for meaning and dynamics. In the case of synch dialogue, for example, you might find thousands of synch points, but only certain ones are important, the ones whose placement defines what we might call the *audiovisual phrasing* of the sequence.

Comparison

It is often illuminating to compare the ways that sound and image behave with respect to a given formal aspect of representation. Take speed for example: sound and image can have contrasting speeds, and this difference can create a subtle complementarity of rhythm. Or consider materials and definition: a hard and detail-filled sound can combine with an unfocused and imprecise image (or the other way round), producing an interesting effect. This kind of comparison can happen only by observing the audio and visual elements separately, using the masking method.

It is also interesting to see how each element plays its part in figuration and narration, and how they complement, contradict, or duplicate each other. For example, distance or scale may emerge as a salient factor: a character might be shown in long shot but her or his voice might be heard in sound closeup, or vice versa. The image may be crammed with narrative details while natural sounds are scanty; alternately, we might observe a spare visual composition with a busy soundtrack. These sorts of contrast tend to be strongly evocative and expressive, even if they are not consciously perceived as such. Generally speaking, the cases where sound brings another type of texture to the image without actually belying the image with conspicuous contradiction-counterpoint are the most highly suggestive.

We can easily see that the kind of structure requiring the greatest training and vigilance to study consciously is the "illusionist" type. Film audiences, intellectuals included, tend to see only the forest and not the trees here, and even criticize such films for their "redundant" sound, where in fact sound and image each contribute very different qualities.

Take a well-known film like Ridley Scott's *Blade Runner*. Few people notice that in some of its crowd scenes a typical shot will contain very few characters, while on the soundtrack one hears a veritable flood of humanity. A good example would be Harrison Ford's pursuit of Joanna Cassidy in the street. The effect of pullulation created in this manner is actually stronger and more convincing than it would be if people were massed in the frame to "match" the numerous voices. Here again we confront problems of "rendering," to which Gombrich's discussion in *Art and Illusion* is wholly relevant.

Finally, *technical* comparison is in order when the framing is modified by camera movements: how does the soundtrack behave in relation to variations in scale and depth? Does the sound ignore these changes, exaggerate them, or accompany them discreetly? This is not so easy to analyze. In any case, no situation is ever "neutral" or "normal," and thereby unworthy of consideration.

The issue of figurative comparison may be condensed into two complementary questions whose deceptive simplicity we must not allow to blind us to the significant revelations they can provide. *What do I see of what I hear?* I hear a street, a train, voices. Are their sources visible? offscreen? suggested visually? *What do I hear of what I see?* This symmetrical question is often difficult to answer well, for the potential sources of sounds in a shot are more numerous than we might ordinarily imagine.

By attending to these kinds of questions we can discover both *negative sounds* in the image (the image calls for them, but the film does not produce them for us to hear) and *negative images* in the sound—"present" solely in the suggestion the soundtrack makes. The sounds that are there, the images that are there often have no other function than artfully outlining the form of these "absent presences," these sounds and images, which, in their very negativity, are often the more important. Cinema's poetry springs from such things.

STRENGTHS AND PITFALLS OF AUDIOVISUAL ANALYSIS: FELLINI'S La Dolce Vita

Audiovisual analysis has its difficulties. I would like to illustrate some of these by citing remarks and observations made by students during an assignment in which they were to do an audio-visual description of a sequence in *La Dolce Vita*. In using these quotations I do not intend to present either a collection of foolish misstatements or a scholarly anthology; instead I wish to show how the method of observation works, and the pitfalls it can encounter.

For our text we used a small segment that runs from the end of the opening credits to a point in the second sequence (the nightclub scene). The first sequence opens with two helicopters flying over Rome on a sunny day. One of them is carrying, suspended, a large statue of Christ with his arms open, the other is transporting the journalist Marcello (Mastroianni) and his paparazzo photographer. The second helicopter hovers for a few moments over a terrace on the roof of a modern building, to flirt, in the din of the copter blades, with high-society women who are sunbathing up there. The second sequence shows Marcello the yellow journalist at work in a chic nightclub, one of whose attractions is an exotic pseudo-Siamese dancing show. There he meets a beautiful, rich, bored woman (Anouk Aimée).

I showed the segment to the students five times, using the masking procedure. They screened it twice with both the sound and image running, once without sound, once with no image, and finally a last time with both sound and image again. Afterward the students had two hours to write an audiovisual analysis based on their notes.

Besides many interesting remarks, I found in their essays a number of phenomena I'll categorize as *retrospective illusion*, which eloquently attest to the workings of added value. For example, some radio music (on-the-air) is heard in the shot of the women tanning on the roof. Certain students described it as "full of life, sun, and joy" or "reminiscent of the beach and the sun," while what's on the soundtrack is a pleasant swing tune with no special characteristics; this music might just as fittingly accompany a shot of a busy street at night. What happened is that the plot situation rubbed off on the music as the students remembered it.

We also find false memories, for example memories of sounds that were only suggested by the image and the general tone of the sequence. In an aerial shot of St. Peter's square crammed with people one student heard the "acclamations of a crowd." This sound does not exist; it was created (as a negative sound) by the sight of the crowd and by the grand chiming of churchbells heard with the image.

In addition, sounds that do exist and are even quite prominent seem to have evaporated in some memories. One student noted an abrupt silence in the shot of the women in bathing suits. He totally blocked out Nino Rota's swing music; apparently all he retained from that moment was the fact that the helicopter's hum is interrupted.

Some students "interpreted" aural fluctuations based on visual movements they observed. Having seen the helicopters very definitely approaching or receding from the camera, many "heard" the sound's volume increase in what they felt was an exact parallel to the image ("the audio world is in exact synch with the shots on the screen"). A few students, however, noticed that the sound in fact "follows" the image much more loosely. They recognized that the *visual respirations* of flying objects increasing and decreasing in screen size are sometimes answered by *audio respirations*, swelling and diminishing of sound, and noted that these two processes do not follow a point-by-point synchronism as much as a principle of deferred propagation (the sound swells early or with a delay with respect to what is seen). It's precisely this time lag that makes everything seem natural, like a series of waves that spread out in intervals.

(Let us note also that in real experience, variation in volume of a moving object is not exactly parallel to its variation in our field of vision either.)

Another student noticed very pertinently that in the sequence "sounds vary with an uneven volume that does not seem to depend exclusively on their distance" (meaning the distance from their sources to the camera).

What is interesting in many essays is the need some students felt to rationalize the modifications and anomalies in the sound-image relationship by attempting mechanically to apply the rule of point of audition to them. If we do not hear a sound implied by the image, they reason, this is because the character in the image is for some reason not hearing it (subjective sense of point of audition), or it has to do with the camera's position (spatial sense of point of audition).

Thus some participants attempted to justify—while they were only asked to describe—variations in volume, by making an ambiguous reference to subjective point of audition. For example, regarding the drowned-out dialogue between the men in the helicopter and the women on the terrace, a student proposed that "our hearing the women's voices but not the men's reflects perhaps that the men are used to the helicopter's sound, and so for them, it has become background, rather than the noisy roar it is for the women." The author of this comment interprets the images of the women (whose voices are heard) as being situated in the men's points of view and audition, and vice versa, even though there is nothing in the text to indicate this. If we judge by the camera positions, much closer to the women than to the men, we would conclude rather that the whole scene is constructed from the female point of view, and so it would be logical that it's the women who hear their own voices, and not the men's voices . . .

So we can see all the ambiguity that inheres in the notion of point of audition (here in its subjective sense).

Regarding the same scene, another student frankly reversed the situation in his memory: "The sound of the women's voices is covered up by the sound of the helicopter." Unless by covered up he means not that the sound is inaudible but that it is partially drowned. The same term can thus mean two completely opposite things, and we can never be too careful about being sufficiently precise, since the rigor of the perception depends strictly on the rigor of language used to describe it.

Since the film involves men and women, and since the first scene shows the sexes in two separate groups, several students were tempted to theorize *La Dolce Vita* from a gender perspective. Some indeed succumbed to their temptation, taking their cue from a line in the nightclub scene: a man says "shut up" to his female companion who has just expressed an opinion. So Fellini depicts a world where "women do not have the right to speak," and he illustrates this, they opine, by not letting women open their mouths during the whole sequence. However, in the same sequence, we see the prince's blonde companion speak to him as she runs her fingers through his hair, and Anouk Aimée also has a good number of lines she speaks to the bartender with the haughtiness of a very rich woman.

Does this mean that audiovisual description must be limited to a sort of inventory of details, shying away from any reading or overall perspective? Certainly not. For the most interesting essays were those that freed themselves from the causal yoke (the soundtrack has X because the image shows Y) in favor of a dynamic analysis—that is, an analysis that takes into account the evolving and changing nature of soundtrack and image in time. One student discerned in the sequence's audiovisual structure a principle of perpetual movement and overlapping. From the outset he grasped this as a general principle, and not event by event. For example, in the first sequence, we hear a group of children's joyous shouts emerging like a wave from under the helicopters' humming, then later the bells of St. Peter's covering and absorbing in its turn the hum of the blades, and so on. According to another student, the dynamics of this overlap pattern resembles wave dynamics. And indeed, the organic quality of a wave's profile presides over the sonic organization of the first sequence.

Appropriately, this scene revolves around a vibrating ovoid object, likely to trace less linear trajectories than an airplane: something that can grow, fly around in all three dimensions, hover in one place, like a living and breathing organism.

The same student who discovered the overlap principle notes that each of the segment's two parts centers around a particular sound: the helicopter's drone in the first and the exotic music of the second. He further notes that while the first main sound, the hum of the propellers, is *mobile*, sound provides a *fixed* reference point in the second, in the form of the nightclub musicians.

A subtle observation, which seems acoustically false: the music in the nightclub in fact changes volume at various points, and fades down as soon as characters open their mouths. But at the same time it feels profoundly right. Why? Because the fluctuations of the helicopter sound in the first part and those of the music in the second do not obey the same logic, nor do they progress in the same direction.

In the first scene sound, and its source that moves in all directions in space, fluctuates according to a logic that seems determined from within. In the second, which is characterized by more traditional dialogue and structure, sound levels decrease by discontinuous thresholds. The changes appear to be imposed on the musical material from without (external logic) when we hear dialogue—as if obeying a change in point of view. Despite changes in volume, the sound of the nightclub music nevertheless remains the audio-spectator's fixed point of reference in the scene. Claude Bailblé would say that the music maintains a constant "weight" throughout. It gives a more or less stable impression of its volume and power, independent of the real acoustic level, and it does not convey internal instability.

Thus, audiovisual analysis is *descriptive* analysis; it should avoid any symbolizing interpretation of a psychoanalytic, psychological, social, or political nature. Interpretation may of course follow, based on the findings of the analysis. Here, for example, it is not the symbolism of water and waves that interests us, but rather the wave as a dynamic model.

MODEL ANALYSIS: THE PROLOGUE SEQUENCE OF BERGMAN'S Persona (1965)

Actor: Jorgen Lindstrom (young Vogler)
Sound credits
Sound engineer: P. O. Pettersson
Boom operator: Lennart Engholm
Mixing: Olle Jakobsson
Music: Lars Johan Werle

Shot Breakdown

A. The Arc-lamp

1. CU of the arc-lamp of a projector, with its two carbon rods igniting. Starting from a black screen, the rods become increasingly brighter; abstract at first, they take on concrete form, then return to abstraction in the intense light.

Sound: A high, sustained pair of notes (in a major 2d) on string or woodwind instrument. Other notes, having started lower, converge toward the first in an ascending glissando. A whole series of glissandi join in a common bundle moving toward a single high note; strident dissonances the louder and nearer they get to it.

B. Projection, Before Stabilizing

Image: details of a beginning of a screening: film starts rolling, projector lamp ignites.

Sound: After loud ripping, scratching, or skidding noise, we hear the regular click of a mechanism with small spasms, and small bursts of disjointed music in cells of one, two, or three notes: dissonant cells (wind instruments in high registers), likened by some spectators to car horns.

2. Subliminal CU: detail of projector.

3. Brief CU: detail of Maltese Cross alternating several times with black.

4. CU: visible edges of the film.

5. CU of the lens from front (overexposed), alternating several times with white.

6. Markings on film leader: "start," a Z, descending numerals.

7. CU of the projector's film-advancing mechanism.

8. Unfocused shot of film loop, seen from the side, moving in little jumps.

9a, 9b, 9c. CU of the projector gate, with flashes of light; three jump-cuts zoom in on the film and images, which are bright white.

C. Animated Film

Image: a short cartoon, which begins, gets stuck, then resumes.

Sound: projector noise; peppy instrumental music in three-quarter time (flute above) in a scratchy recording (not much treble, light bleeding) playing in a loop like a broken record.

10. The image is less overexposed now, and we see the film: an old animated cartoon projected upside down, showing a chunky woman at the beach leaning over into the water, obsessively washing herself.

11. CU: side view of the film, unfocused.

12. CU: the film running, seen from the other side, unfocused.

13. CU (photographic, not animated) of children's hands,

chubby and white, which duplicate the action of the woman bather, on a black background. This shot (11 and 12 also) is not marked by a specific sound; the projector sound continues.

D. Chaotic Little Film in One Portion of the Screen

Image: a slapstick film in the style of a primitive chase film. It occupies only a portion of the screen; the rest is white.

Sound: various percussion instruments probably including woodblocks or higher register of xylophone; rhythmic, fragmentary, dynamic, with reverberation. The projector noise has disappeared.

14. White screen, over the last of the projector noise.

15. White image, with a sort of "subscreen" appearing in the lower right-hand corner. In the style of the old burlesque silent movies a man in a nightshirt, vintage 1900, is pursued by a skeleton that has jumped out of a trunk.

Three successive shots in the "subscreen": (a) the man turns his back to the trunk where the skeleton popped out; man and skeleton have at one another; man flees from the frame. (b) Man comes out again from the right front, approaches a table from where another figure emerges like a jack-in-the-box. Man flees, and (c) he jumps onto a wrought-iron bed as if he were diving into the water.

16. White screen.

E. Traumatic Images

Image: different visions inscribed in a white halo (antithesis of the sharp edges of the image in the preceding sequence).

Sound: atonal instrumental figures (wind and string instruments) based on sustained but harmonically unstable sounds, with no regular rhythm, with espressivo variations in intensity, everything bathed in reverb. Over the end of shot 19 a rushed and cataclysmic musical figure, Schoenberg style.

17. Burn-in to CU of a black spider. The sound (in lower registers) arrives after the image of the spider.

18. White screen.

19. CU of the fleece of a bleeding sheep. The image has started from a cut; it is irised in white. A man's hands, lit in patches by sun, are squeezing or pressing wool, and blood emerges at length, flowing in silence. Toward the end of the shot the flow is more spasmodic. Piano and other timbres, upward and downward glissandi in strings.

20. Cut to CU, with movement and confusion, of the sheep's eye, zoom in; hands are holding the head steady and move a thumb to its eye. Low note. Agitated tremolo.

21. Confused CU: hands holding a knife slicing organs.

22. Unfocused gray roundness, actually organs, the image irised in white.

The tremolo continues over these two shots (both irised) of hands handling animal entrails.

23. White screen. Higher orchestra note in agitated tremolo, grows louder and will end on a violent point of synchronization (an effect copied directly from the famous B of Alban Berg's *Wozzeck*).[1]

F. Nailed Hand

Image and sound: These three slightly different shots are like different takes of a shot (jump cuts). With the three sounds accompanying the three blows, we have the first true audiovisual synchronism of the sequence, like three powerful chords.

The nailed hand with its palm upward is being grasped at the wrist by another hand. The fingers close as if reflexively when the nail is hammered in.

The shots are again full-frame here, with high-contrast light values.

24. ECU of the nail half in. Very small time delay between image and sound; we hear the dry fortissimo orchestra chord the tremolo built up to and also the noise of the hammer's strike.

25. ECU of the second blow, different angle, with a second pounding noise.

26. ECU, same angle as shot 24: the nail deeper in. The sound is synchronized and slightly lower than the first two. On the third blow, the fingers close gently, then open slowly like a flower, the resistance gone. Relatively long silence when the fingers close and open, silent spasm of the hand.

G. Town

Image: static views of an exterior setting, absolutely without movement.

Sound: distant ringing of churchbells, at first low, muted, and slow, then, behind them, higher slightly more frequent bells.

27. Texture of a surface: wood?

28. Dissolve to long shot of trees in a park: the ground is bare.

29. Cut to close shot of a wrought-iron fence, from oblique angle.

30. Cut to longer shot of a pile of dirty snow (as if piled up by road crews); the fence from shot 29 is in the background.

H. The Dead

Image: Faces and inert parts of men's and women's bodies, which give us to understand that they are dead.

Sound: Slow rhythmic dripping of water (possibly a leaking faucet) heard up close and other sonic events as specified below.

31. ECU: face, horizontal, in profile, toothless mouth, chin.

32. CU: woman's face, very old; a sound of movement nearby, like an animal.

33. LS: body of a small boy lying covered by a sheet as if under a shroud, against a white wall—his body is immobile, only his head and shoulders stick out.

34. ECU (low-angle shot) of a hand, backlit, hanging immobile from a table.

Over shots 33 and 34 are heard approaching footsteps, firm and definite.

35. ECU: face (same woman as shot 32) from another angle; the footsteps are going away.

36. ECU: face of a bald old man, a white sheet on the neck. Over this, just about as we cut to his face, distant noises that sound like a gate being pushed and then two sounds of door(s) closing.

37. ECU: pair of dead person's clasped hands on top of a sheet.

38. ECU: pair of feet in profile; a faraway telephone rings; a second ringing, more insistent. During second ring, cut to:

39. ECU: face of the dead woman, eyes closed, shot from above so that face is upside-down on screen. A third ring begins, and plays over the jump cut to

40. Brief ECU: same face but with eyes wide open.

41. LS: the boy, as in shot 33. Fourth phone ring, shorter and more reverb, at the end of which, after having turned his face toward the camera as if toward the source of the ringing (this is the first movement within the frame since shot 26), the child turns his back to camera and gets under the sheet again, like a sleeper who's been awakened too early in the morning.

Sounds of sheets—all this now seems like a return to the ordinary. Then the boy sits up like someone who can't get back to sleep and lies down again on his stomach. His feet protrude from under the sheet. He raises his head again, gets out of the sheet. He's only in undershorts. The dripping water can still be heard.

42. MCU: head of the boy, with some makeup. He turns his head from the left toward us.

On the soundtrack more hurried footsteps, nearer than before; the boy does not react to them.

Then, still on his bed, the boy looks downward, sees something and leans toward it, leaning on his elbows. The camera follows him. He picks up a pair of glasses from offscreen, puts them on, picks up a book, looks at the cover page (a title in Swedish), uselessly puts the sheet around himself as if he were cold, and opens the book in the middle. At that moment we hear a "frisson" of music (a reprise of some music from the "Traumatic Images" section), which seemingly motivates him to turn his head from right to left, but without any expression of worry. His face in fact hasn't registered any emotion since the beginning.

The child seems to follow the musical phrase in space with his eyes, like a moving form—as if the time of the music were unfolding in space.

Once this music is over he turns back toward the camera with a determined air. His mouth opens a little. He is framed in MCU; he seems to scrutinize something, advances his right hand toward the camera. His hand, moving back and forth, "touches the screen" (in his eyeglasses, we see the reflection of a lamp or a window).

I. The Face

43. MCU: the boy from the rear, his right hand in front of him caressing a white surface (this shot is a reverse-shot of the preceding one, and the only reverse-shot of the sequence).

Sound: returns to the complex of sounds heard at the beginning, this time all centered around one wavering tone in crescendo rather than glissandi, a crescendo that seems to move toward an explosion.

A woman's face seems to form under the boy's fingers (in a process shot), filling most of the frame. It dissolves, reappears differently, becomes Bibi Andersson or Liv Ullmann, and takes on a more or less definite expression. At the end the face closes its eyes via a dissolve—like the inverse of shots 39–40 of the dead woman.

The bundle of tones is more insistent, seems to announce a catastrophe that approaches . . .

Outline for an Audiovisual Analysis

LOCATING THE DOMINANTS

The most obvious thing about the sound is the absence of speech, or any voices for that matter. We have here a portion of a sound film without speech. What remains? Noises, and what may be called music.

The noises may be divided into *lasting noises* (which extend through the whole of a sequence: these include the clicking of the projector, the ringing of churchbells, and the dripping water), and *punctual noises* (isolated events: for example, the hammer blows, the footsteps in the mortuary, the swishing of sheets). The lasting noises ensure some continuity in the sequences they occupy by linking shots that are extremely disparate in appearance, texture, and content.

As for music, the question of whether it is clearly identifiable as such (as distinct from noise) depends on the listener's cultural references. For example, the initial bundle of glissandi over shot 1 will be identified as music by those whose background permits them to recognize string instruments, and also a kind of sliding sound typical of contemporary music, while for others it might signify little more than a sirenlike noise. Of course, the same listener can recognize in these initial sounds both their probable instrumental source and their form of siren sound with absolutely no contradiction.

This necessarily reminds us that the distinction between music and noise is completely relative, and has to do with what we are listening for.

LOCATING POINTS OF SYNCHRONIZATION

Synch points in the prologue are both rare and striking. At first glance the sequence hardly seems to have any. For example, they occur extremely subtly and infrequently in the mortuary sequence—at the very most, slight sounds of sheets when the boy turns over in bed. The "traumatic images" section is entirely asynchronous, in the sense that there are no sounds that coincide with precise visual moments.

The most vivid synch points are obviously the three violent hammer blows into the hand. Note that the the film prepares for them not only by the orchestral crescendo that builds up to them but also by the entire preceding sequence, which envelops us in a sort of asynchronous fog of images and sounds where nothing has distinct outlines in either space or time.

On the other hand, the double flow that characterizes the whole beginning—the visual flow of the projected images and the sonic flow of the sewing-machinelike projector noise, includes tight synch points, which stitch the two together in simultaneous spasms and interruptions of continuity. Likewise the triple-time music, which starts with the movements of the cartoon bather, pauses with her, and resumes when she begins moving again.

So we can see different modes of synchronization at work. At the start sound and image are treated like two parallel lines that have peaks and dips in concert; while over the three hammer strikes we note a very vertical and specific moment, quite detached from the rest. In the first case the synch points accentuate the effect of horizontality (insistence on a flow, even an uneven one), and in the second they emphasize verticality (insistence on a unique and irreversible moment).

Narrative Analysis

A sound-image comparison is also in order on the level of narration and figuration. To do this we might start by asking, *What do I hear of what I see?* and *What do I see of what I hear?*

It becomes quite clear that the moment of the hammer blows is central, not just because of the traumatic impact of the event depicted. It's also because this is the only moment during which we unambiguously *audio-view*, in image and in sound, the same thing at the same moment and on the same level of reality.

Despite its apparent realism, the entire mortuary sequence derives its strangeness from the scarcity of synch points. We should note that the situation in itself (inert bodies, a silent reclining child, an interior, a peaceful moment) does not imply many movements and, accordingly, not many sounds either. In addition, almost everything is shot in closeups, which drastically reduce the number of objects visible in each frame. Also if we hear very little of what we see . . . there isn't much there that can move!

The sound of sequence H involves very active elements, like that indescribable brushing sound at the beginning of the sequence in shot 32 (it could be an animal furtively bolting or some human movement), and especially the brusque footsteps.

But we never see the source of this sound or the owner of the footsteps, just as we don't see the faucet that drips steadily.

(Let us also note the strategy adopted regarding auditory *extension*: the soundtrack isolates us quickly from exterior sounds when we "enter" the mortuary. From this point onward we hear neither birds nor cars nor the churchbells of the preceding sequence, which resonate only over the beginning of the first shot in sequence H in order to establish temporal continuity and to interconnect the exteriors glimpsed in sequence G and this interior, to which the rest of the prologue is henceforth confined.)

What concretely links sound to image in this sequence is thus pointedly minimal. On one hand, it's the subtle noises of bedclothes accompanying the boy's movements. On the other, some of the child's gestures seem to be responding to something happening on the soundtrack, although we cannot be certain.

For example, when the telephone rings repeatedly, we see the child, until then as still as a cadaver, stir in his bed: we then figure that he is reacting to the sound and is going to answer. But a moment later he resumes his place as if to go back to sleep. So not only does he turn out not to be concerned by the ringing, but nothing in the image clearly designates that he has even heard it.

Still more mysterious: the lateral movement of his eyes seems to match the movement of the music cue (taken from the "traumatic images" sequence). It is impossible to tell whether he sees something of what we hear, not to mention whether he "hears" it at all—or else whether it's a pure coincidence. The music here is very interesting: it does not serve conventionally to "accompany" what is going on in the image, but acts as a phenomenon unto itself, a pure sonic event whose status in the represented reality we strive to understand.

Surely there is an overall narrative coherence between what we see and what we hear (the dripping faucet and the officious footsteps "go well" with the idea of a mortuary, and silence goes with the sight of cadavers), but in the details there remains a mysterious ambivalence. The spectator must do a lot of projecting, onto the image as well as the sound, since nothing is explicitly shown, much less named.

As I stated at the beginning of this book, added value functions in its pure state when we see the lifeless faces. The film presents totally inert and atemporal images, which only the sound of drops of water inscribes into a linear diegetic time. Without sound, this would merely be a series of photographic stills in mutual isolation.

But this Bergman sequence, which I have chosen as a kind of pedagogical limit-case of sound-image experimentation, also poses questions about the narrativity of sound per se. The questions are complex and too difficult to answer conclusively here, but we must not hesitate to formulate them nonetheless.

For example, regarding what I have been calling the drops of water, solely on the faith of my ears, neither seeing dripping liquid nor having other sensory proof: what tells me that I'm hearing water, and not blood, or some other liquid for that matter?

If we think *water*, it is because experience has led us to associate a certain sort of sound with a particular consistency. A thicker liquid—blood or milk—does not produce the same sound when it drips. We also think of water because the rhythm of these isolated sound impulses, at once periodic and very slightly irregular, conjures up a leaky faucet more readily than, say, a leaking bottle or a human body being emptied of its blood. The subtle resonance around each impulse can conceivably correspond to a container like a sink.

Thus extremely disparate factors are at work in aiding our identification of the source. We recognize (or think we recognize) a sound as coming from a certain source based both on its form

and timbre, which we may check against our memory's dictionary of recognizable sounds (a fairly small dictionary at that).
Our identification of the sound source is then reinforced insofar
as the situation in the film logically would call for it. Recognition,
therefore, is based on both internal qualities of sound and factors
external to the sound.

The rhythm of the dripping water in the film can be characterized as fairly calm, but not calming. By nature this periodic sound
captures our attention and keeps it on guard, to the point of exas-
peration, because each repetition occurs slightly "off" the
moment when we're awaiting it. It thus creates a "texture of presentness" that is rather tense, even intense.

The footsteps, for their part, illustrate the narrative indeterminacy proper to sound: we recognize a human step, but we have
no precise image of the person walking, even whether it's a man
or woman. Some might say that the determined and emphatic
quality of the step, detectable in its rhythm and timbre, point to a
man, but isn't this a rather sexist stereotype? Is there no feminine
gait that is firm and decisive?

The sense of resolve in the gait confers to this offscreen sound
its everyday professional air: it is not a theatrical step, of the sort
that evokes a character's entry onstage.

The treatment of these sounds of footsteps and dripping suggests a place where death is a common everyday phenomenon.

COMPARISON

We may compare image and sound in many capacities; a good
start will be in terms of forms and textures.

At the beginning of the segment, the image is full of violent
contrasts and cuts, convulsive movements, sharp visual contours,
and strong lighting. It is no accident that the soundtrack offers the

same sharp and precise quality, marked by abrupt and noticeable attacks and by the relative absence of reverb (which has a tendency to "dilute" and soften sound contours). The sequence of "traumatic images" also features audiovisual solidarity between the blurred quality of the image's contours and values (haloing) and the underwaterish, gummy quality of the music. The latter is created in different ways: by the musical style itself (atonal, producing an effect of vagueness), by the form of the sounds (soft attacks, progressive variations in intensity), and by characteristics of auditory space (very strong reverb around the sounds). So in these two cases, image and sound are mutually reinforced through identity of texture and form.

The silent chase film presents a more ambiguous case for sound-image comparison. The movements in this scene inside the insert-screen are jerky and spasmodic, just as the percussive music heard over it consists entirely of nonpatterned sounds and irregular, almost out-of-joint rhythms. And yet the sound of this music is "sweetened" and blurred by considerable reverberation.

In this short sequence the spectator has an *impression* of synchronization points, for she or he can't help but be aware of discontinuity and nonpatterned sounds and images. At the same time Bergman has taken care not to synchronize the audio and visual channels point by point. Their relation has an aleatory quality, from moment to moment as well as in the scene's general progression. Any synch points remain imagined and projected by the spectator, who is thereby prepared for the very real and brutal ones to come, those of the hammered hand.

In her study of *Persona* Marilyn Johns Blackwell speaks of the sounds here "crescendo[ing] as the action accelerates," postulating a sort of convergence or common movement in the audio and visual tracks, thus a tendency toward resynchronization.[2] Even though no such thing exists, total disorder with no apparent goal is intolerable for human beings. We cannot resist giving it structure and form, a teleology, a shape and direction, even when it itself has none (we have imposed this very tendency to order on the aleatory arrangement of the stars in the sky).

THE AUDIOVISUAL CANVAS

We begin to notice the categories of contrast and opposition among the various sequences: jerky-smooth, sharp-diffuse, regular-irregular, ordered-disorderly.

Smoothness is represented in the prologue by . . . one sound less: the disappearance of the spasmodic sewing-machine sound of the projector. The projector sound's general irregularity and tremoloesque microtexture (a dense and infinitesimally irregular vibration) serve as materializing indices, evoking a slightly rickety machine. So its disappearance gives the feeling that the projection is moving smoothly from now on. (Likewise, a TV car commercial will create the impression of a silky-smooth engine by cutting out the sound of the motor from shots of the car driving on a highway.)

If we wished to characterize the overall dynamic of this prologue, we could also invoke the psychophysiological phenomenon of the *spasm*, a sudden contraction interrupting the normal tension of a muscle. In the image, when blood spurts from the animal being bled, it flows straight down but also quivers. In the sound, the strings play a tremolo, clearly shaped but quivering in its microtexture. In each case the overall logic consists of an implacable and well-defined movement, while in its detail it is agitated and quivering.

This dynamic of the spasm can be seen in relation to the fact that the idea of touching, of tactility, appears obsessively throughout the sequence.[3] We can see it directly, with concrete images of hands (the bather's, the child's, the man's holding the bleeding animal), as well as indirectly, with the shots of the spider, the lamb fleece, and of course in the insistence on the visual proximity of extreme closeups. The film stock itself trembles like a tactile surface.

We should also note the tight construction of this prologue whose beginning and end engage the same process: an image that's undecided or erratic in itself onto which the soundtrack imprints a powerful dramatization by means of a very intentional and insistent crescendo. On both occasions something seems to get more and more precise, whether by the increasing brightness at the beginning or by the hope of seeing a clear face emerge at the end. So each involves the idea of revelation, of epiphany, associated with the hope for a convergence of the two logics of sound and image, toward an absolute point where the two will dissolve together. The beginning segment strives toward Absolute light in Absolute noise; for the end, Absolute sound and Absolute "exchange of looks."

In between these framing segments are two sequences where sound and image flee from one another, subtly avoid each other, without overtly contradicting each other. The two sequences are separated at their center by three vigorous and traumatizing points of synchronization, each prepared by a sonic crescendo. The synch points constitute an event in itself (independent of plot content), a pure event of audiovisual mise-en-scène.

By means of the various processes we have enumerated, Bergman seems to wish to stretch to the maximum what I have called the "audiovisual canvas," at the same time seeking to grasp what this tension creates, on its surface, in terms of an almost panicky quivering, an uncontrollable epidermal agitation. And the three points of synchronization are like the three stakes that support this canvas, for cinematic representation, in audiovisual space.

NOTES

1. PROJECTIONS OF SOUND ON IMAGE

1. Chion's terminology, referring as it does to the register of political economy, is based on a pun: *value added by text* plays on the *value added tax* imposed on purchases of goods and services in France and the rest of the EC.—TRANS.

2. Léon Zitrone: French TV anchor, a household word in France since the early years of television. Zitrone did commentary for horse races, figure skating, official ceremonies such as royal weddings, and air shows.

3. Pascal Bonitzer, *Le Regard et la voix*, pp. 37–40. See also the opening of chapter 8, on film sound, in David Bordwell and Kristin Thompson, *Film Art: An Introduction*.

4. Michel Chion, *Le Son au cinéma*, chapter 7, "La Belle Indifférente," pp. 119–42, especially pp. 122–26.

5. Throughout this book I use the phrase *audiovisual contract* as a

reminder that the audiovisual relationship is not natural, but a kind of symbolic contract that the audio-viewer enters into, agreeing to think of sound and image as forming a single entity.

6. Here by *density* I mean the density of sound events. A sound with marked and rapid modifications in a given time will temporally animate the image in a different way than a sound that varies less in the same time.

2. THE THREE LISTENING MODES

1. English lacks words for two French terms: *le regard*, the fact or mode of looking, which has been translated in film theory as both "the look" and "the gaze," and its aural equivalent, *l'écoute*. Here, *l'écoute* alternately appears in English as as "mode of listening" and "listening."—TRANS.

2. Linguistics distinguishes perception of meaning from perception of sound by establishing the different categories of phonetics, phonology, and semantics.

3. Pierre Schaeffer, *Traité des objets musicaux*, p. 270, and Michel Chion, *Guide des objets sonores*, p. 33. The adjective "reduced" is borrowed from Husserl's phenomenological notion of reduction.

4. See Rick Altman on the "sound hermeneutic," in "Moving Lips," pp. 67–79.—TRANS.

3. LINES AND POINTS: HORIZONTAL AND VERTICAL PERSPECTIVES ON AUDIOVISUAL RELATIONS

1. For an excellent essay on this topic, see David Bordwell, "The Musical Analogy."—TRANS.

2. Chion, *La voix au cinéma*, pp. 13–14.

3. Talk given in 1937, and cited by Henri Colpi in his excellent book, *Défense et illustration de la musique dans le film*.

4. Chion, *Le Son au cinéma*, p. 106.

5. Chion, *La Toile trouée*, pp. 11–15.

6. In one of Hill's videos, *Primarily Speaking* (1981–83), images are edited in exact synch with the articulation of syllables in a spoken text uttered as a voiceover.

4. THE AUDIOVISUAL SCENE

Chion's French title for this chapter is "La Scène audio-visuelle." By scène *he means "stage" or "scenic space."*—TRANS.

1. This preexisting frame I speak of is not exactly the one to which Pascal Bonitzer and Jacques Aumont refer in opposing the cinematic frame to that of painting. See Bonitzer, *Décadrages*, and Aumont, *L'Image*.

2. See my comments on this in chapter 5 of *Le Son au cinéma*, p. 91.

3. See Rick Altman, "The Material Heterogeneity of Recorded Sound," p. 24.

4. For analysis of sound perspective, see Rick Altman, "Sound Space," in Altman, ed., *Sound Theory/Sound Practice*, pp. 46–64; also, in the same volume, Steve Wurtzler, " 'She Sang Live But the Microphone Was Turned Off': The Live, the Recorded, and the Subject of Representation," pp. 87–103, especially pp. 96–99.—TRANS.

5. Schaeffer, *Traité des objets musicaux*, pp. 91–99.

6. Consider for example the streetcar bell in Bresson's *A Man Escaped*, which I analyzed in *Le Son au cinéma*.

7. See Michel Marie's book in the Synopsis series, *M le Maudit* (Paris: Editions Nathan), Francis Vanoye, general editor.

8. Odile Larère, *De l'imaginaire au cinéma*.

9. That is, situated in another time and another place than the events directly represented.

10. For one solution to this question, see Bordwell and Thompson's category of "internal diegetic sound," in chapter 8 of *Film Art: An Introduction*.—TRANS.

11. See chapter 3 of Chion, *La Voix au cinéma*.

12. *Passe-muraille*: a person who can walk through walls. The expression comes from a Kafkaesque tale by Marcel Aymé, a sad story of a man who discovered that he could go through walls. His gift led to his downfall; he lost it at the very moment of passing through a wall, and was trapped inside.

13. See my analysis of this film in the chapter of *La Toile trouée* entitled "Une petite pointe de lumière rouge" (a small spot of red light).

14. Interview with Walter Murch, *Positif* (1989), no. 338.

15. Simultaneous, and not successive as for images.

16. Chion's "scotomization" comes from the medical term "scotoma": obscuration of part of the visual field, or the condition of having blind spots, caused by defects in the brain or retina.—TRANS.

5. THE REAL AND THE RENDERED

1. Which I described in *Le Son au cinéma*, pp. 71–72.

2. By dualistic I mean that these films play on the division of the character into two parts, consonant with the philosophical dualism of body and soul: the voice on the soundtrack, the visible aspect in the image.

3. English-speaking readers might want to think of Kevin Costner or Meryl Streep.—TRANS.

4. *Notebooks of Leonardo Da Vinci*, sec. 10, 1:280.

5. Despite beginnings of an undertaking of naming and classification, which is encountering healthy resistance.

6. François Delalande and Bernadette Céleste, *L'Enfant: Du sonore au musical*.

6. PHANTOM AUDIO-VISION

Phantom *here is used like the medical term* phantom pain, *as an approximation of Chion's phrase* en creux. En creux *properly refers to negative space—the shape of the space in a sculptor's mold, defined by the mold. In this chapter Chion is negotiating the territory of transference from one sensory channel to another, which sometimes produces psychological "presences" in the face of perceptual "absences." This translation uses both "negative" and "phantom" for* en creux. *See also Walter Murch's introduction, which translates* en creux *as "in the gap."*—TRANS.

1. Maurice Merleau-Ponty, *Phénoménologie de la perception*, 2:368.

2. Acousmêtre: a portmanteau word coined by Chion based on two French words, *acousmatique* (acousmatic, see chapter 4) and *être* (being). -TRANS. Chion, *La Voix au cinéma*, pp. 25–33.

3. Some recent comedies, such as Woody Allen's *Alice* and Jerry Zucker's *Ghost*, hint at the birth of a new family of acousmêtres.

4. That is, there is no one-on-one deterministic relationship between the organs called eye or ear, and the perceptions called image or sound.

7. SOUND FILM—WORTHY OF THE NAME

1. With the term *superchamp*, Chion is describing a new and vaster space beyond the merely offscreen (*hors-champ*). The term is translated as "superfield," rather than "superscreen."—TRANS.

2. When sound is more and more frequently in long shot, the image tends to differentiate itself from the soundtrack on the level of scale—i.e., there are more closeups. I call this a spontaneous phenomenon because I think it has developed without a great deal of conscious intellectual thought. As for the tendency to complementarity: the idea is that in the combining of auditory long shots and visual closeups, image and sound do not create an effect of contrast, opposition and dissonance, but rather an effect of complementarity. They bring different points of view to a same scene.

3. Particularly at the beginning of *Wings of Desire*, the numerous characters' internal voices, and Peter Handke's literary text ("Als das Kind Kind war . . . "), are clearly inspired from the Hörspiel tradition, a form of radio composition that used the human voice and text often in very complex ways.

8. TELEVISION, VIDEO ART, MUSIC VIDEO

1. Chion, *La Toile trouée*, pp. 111–15.

9. TOWARD AN AUDIOLOGOVISUAL POETICS

1. A shortened version of this chapter appears as the article "Wasted Words," translated by Rick Altman, in the anthology *Sound Theory/Sound Practice*, also edited by Altman. I have used Altman's terms for the three kinds of speech, and I am also indebted to him for other details of this translation.—TRANS.

2. See below, "The Wandering Text."

3. Camera and voiceover wander along seemingly separate trajectories, until for example, Godard pronounces the word *water* and suddenly we see the water of Lake Leman. The viewer gets the impression that the commentary and images have found each other, if only temporarily.

4. Anglophone readers might think of Robert Altman's films for obvious cases of emanation speech.—TRANS.

5. A parallel image shows something different from what the dialogue is about, without being contradictory. Hitchcock's films have scenes showing characters embracing tenderly while saying banal or even vulgar lines; think, for example, of James Stewart and Grace Kelly at the beginning of *Rear Window*. A contradictory image of the embracing couple might have them say they hate each other. The senses of the image and of the dialogue would be frankly opposed.

6. Such an operation would be even easier during postsynchronization.

10. INTRODUCTION TO AUDIOVISUAL ANALYSIS

1. In act 3 of *Wozzeck*, between scenes 2 and 3, the orchestra, which has been playing with a considerable complexity of voices, comes together in unison on a B. The single note swells in a huge crescendo, and then suddenly cuts off. At that moment the stage lighting changes suddenly and the audience sees the setting of a cabaret. At the same time the music changes to an out of tune cabaret piano playing.

2. Marilyn Johns Blackwell, *Persona: The Transcendent Image*, p. 18. "This shot [shot 15] is performed in the jerky fast motion of old films and is accompanied by bangs and wooden crashes which crescendo as the action accelerates."

3. Physically speaking a spasm is a nervous phenomenon, usually manifested by epidermal quiverings. I think that in Bergman there is something epidermal to the spasmodic agitation; there is a connection to skin, which he often shows very close up.

GLOSSARY

Acousmatic: Pertaining to sound one hears without seeing its source. Radio and telephone are acousmatic media. In a film, an offscreen sound is acousmatic.

Acousmêtre (from *acousmatic* and *être* ["being"]): A kind of voice-character specific to cinema that in most instances of cinematic narratives derives mysterious powers from being heard and not seen. See acousmêtres in *The Invisible Man*, *1000 Eyes of Dr Mabuse*, *The Wizard of Oz*.

Added value: The expressive and/or informative value with which a sound enriches a given image, so as to create the definite impression (either immediate or remembered) that this meaning emanates "naturally" from the image itself.

Anempathetic sound: Sound—usually diegetic music—that seems to exhibit conspicuous indifference to what is going on in the film's plot, creating a strong sense of the tragic. For example, a radio continues to play a happy tune even as the character who first turned it on has died.

The opposite of *empathetic*—sound (again, usually music) whose mood matches the mood of the action.

Audiovisual contract: The audiovisual relationship is not natural but rather a sort of symbolic pact to which the audio-spectator agrees when she or he considers the elements of sound and image to be participating in one and the same entity or world.

Back voice: A person's voice heard from the perspective of the back of the person. If his or her back is turned, the listener perceives less treble in the voice. See also *frontal voice*.

Causal listening: Listening for the purpose of gaining information about the sound's source. See also *semantic listening, reduced listening*.

Elements of auditory setting (E.A.S.): Distinct, intermittent, localized sounds that flesh out and give individuality to a scene's setting.

Emanation speech: A use of speech found infrequently in films, wherein the words are not completely heard or understood. Speech becomes a sort of emanation of the characters, not essential for understanding significant action or meaning. See also *textual speech, theatrical speech*.

Empathetic music: Music whose mood or rhythm matches with the mood or rhythm of the action onscreen. See *anempathetic*.

Extension of the (diegetic) sound space: the degree of openness or largeness of the cinematic space suggested by the sounds. In *null extension* the sonic universe is shrunken to the sounds heard by a single character. In *vast extension* there is as nearly infinite a dilation of the sonic space as possible.

External logic: The logic by which the flow of sound includes effects of discontinuity as nondiegetic interventions. See also *internal logic*.

Frontal voice: A person's voice heard from a frontal perspective. See also *back voice*.

In-the-wings effect: In multitrack cinema, sound lingering in lateral speakers after the exit of a character, automobile, etc. from the screen, or arising there before the character or object comes onscreen. This literally offscreen sound encourages the audio-viewer to believe that the character or object is there in the space just offscreen. This effect was generally eliminated after the early period of multitrack sound.

Internal logic: The logic by which the sound flow is apparently born out of the narrative situation itself. See *external logic*.

Internal sound: Diegetic sound that corresponds to the physical and/or mental interior of a character, e.g., heartbeats, voices imagined or recollected.

Magnetization (spatial): Mental spatialization; the psychological process (in monaural film viewing) of locating a sound's source in the space of the image, no matter what the real point of origin of the sound in the viewing space is, e.g., one will mentally place a voice as coming from offscreen left, in tandem with visual indications about the person speaking, even though the sound really emanates from a speaker behind the center of the screen.

Materializing sound indices (m.s.i.): Sonic details that supply information about the concrete materiality of sound production in the film space, e.g., a pianist's breathing and fingernails on the piano keys. Sparse m.s.i.s give the impression of perfection, ethereality, abstraction.

Negative sound: See *phantom sound*. Chion's French term is *en creux*, which translates as "negative space" (in sculpture, the volume defined by the mould). See also Walter Murch's introduction, which translates *en creux* as "in the gap."

Offscreen trash: An effect of multitrack sound film: as a crash or other loud event occurs visually in the middle of the screen, one hears participatory sounds in the lateral and surround speakers.

On-the-air sound: Sound heard in a film narrative that is supposedly transmitted by radio, television, telephone, or another electronic source and that consequently is not subject to "natural" laws of sound propagation.

Pit music: Nondiegetic music. The term refers analogically to the space of the orchestra pit with respect to the drama or spectacle on stage. See also *screen music*.

Phantom (body, audio-vision, sound): As in *phantom pain*, a "false" perception based on formal expectations, on psychological rather than physical stimulus.

Point of synchronization or *synch point*: Audiovisually salient synchronous meeting of a sound event and a sight event. Example: a dramatic cut in both image and soundtrack, sound effect or striking musical note or cadence, or emphasized word of dialogue, coinciding with an action, a zoom in, etc.

Reduced listening: Listening for the purpose of focusing on the qualities of the sound itself (pitch, timbre, etc.) independent of its source or meaning. See also *causal listening* and *semantic listening*.

Rendering: The use of sounds to convey the feelings or effects associated with the situation on screen—often in opposition to faithful *reproduction* of the sounds that might be heard in the situation in reality. Rendering frequently translates an agglomerate of sensations. For example, sound accompanying a fall is often a great crash, conveying weight, violence, and pain.

Screen music: Music that apparently arises from a source in the space/time of the story, diegetic music. See also *pit music*.

Semantic listening: Listening for the purpose of gaining information about what is communicated in the sound (usually language). See also *reduced listening* and *causal listening*.

Spatial magnetization: See *magnetization*.

Superfield: The sound space created by multitrack sound and multi-speaker placement in the movie theater.

Synch point: See *point of synchronization*.

Synchresis: The forging of an immediate and necessary relationship between something one sees and something one hears at the same time (from *synchronism* and *synthesis*). The psychological phenomenon of synchresis is what makes dubbing and much other postproduction sound mixing possible.

Territory sounds: Ambient sounds whose pervasive presence gives definition to a space, e.g., bird songs, churchbells.

Textual speech: Speech in a film having the power to make visible the images that it evokes. Infrequent, and usually limited to one character. See also *emanation speech, theatrical speech*.

Theatrical speech: The most common use of speech in film, wherein characters exchange dialogue that is integrally heard by the spectator. See also *emanation speech, textual speech*.

BIBLIOGRAPHY

Altman, Rick. "Moving Lips: Cinema as Ventriloquism." In Rick Altman, ed., "Cinema/Sound," special issue, *Yale French Studies* (1980), no. 60.

———— "The Technology of the Voice." In "Speech in Film," special issue of *Iris* (1985), vol. 3, no. 1.

———— "L'Espace sonore." In *Histoire du cinéma: nouvelles approches*. Colloque de Cerisy/Sorbonne, 1989.

———— "The Material Heterogeneity of Recorded Sound," In Rick Altman, ed., *Sound Theory/Sound Practice*. New York: Routledge, 1992.

———— "Sound Space," In Rick Altman, ed., *Sound Theory/Sound Practice*. New York: Routledge, 1992.

Altman, Rick, ed. "Cinema/Sound." Special issue. *Yale French Studies* (1980), no. 60.

———— *Sound Theory/Sound Practice*. New York: Routledge, 1992.

Aumont, Jacques. *L'Image*. Paris: Nathan, 1990.

Aumont, Jacques and Michel Marie, *L'Analyse des films*, Paris: Nathan-Université, 1988.

Bailblé, Claude, Michel Marie, and Marie-Claire Ropars-Wuilleumier, "Un film sonore, un film musical, un film parlant." In *Muriel: histoire d'une recherche*, Paris: Galilée, 1974.

Bandy, M. L. ed. *The Dawn of Sound*. New York: Museum of Modern Art, 1989.

Bayle, Francis. "La musique acousmatique." In *Encyclopaedia Universalis: Symposium*, p. 211. Paris: Encyclopaedia Universalis, 1989.

Belaygue, Christian, ed. *Le Passage du muet au parlant*. Toulouse: Cinémathèque de Toulouse/Editions Milan, 1988.

Blackwell, Marilyn Johns. *Persona: The Transcendent Image*. Chicago: University of Illinois Press, 1986.

Bonitzer, Pascal. *Le Regard et la voix*, Paris: Union Générale d'Editions, 1976.

——— *Décadrages: Le cinéma dans la peinture*. Paris: Cahiers du cinéma, 1985.

Bordwell, David. "The Musical Analogy." In "Cinema/Sound," *Yale French Studies* (1980), no. 60, pp. 141–56.

Bordwell, David and Kristin Thompson. *Film Art: An Introduction*. 4th ed. New York: McGraw-Hill, 1993.

Burch, Noel. *Theory of Film Practice*. New York: Praeger, 1973.

——— *To the Distant Observer: Form and Meaning in the Japanese Cinema*. Berkeley: University of California Press, 1979.

Chion, Michel. *Le Cinéma comme art sonore*. 3 vols. Paris: Cahiers du cinéma. *La Voix au cinéma*, 1982; *Le Son au cinéma*, 1985; *La Toile trouée, la parole au cinéma*, 1988.

——— *Jacques Tati*. Paris: Cahiers du cinéma, 1987.

——— *Guide des objets sonores*. Paris: INA/Buchet-Chastel, 1983.

Delalande, François and Bernadette Céleste. *L'Enfant: Du sonore au musical*. Paris: INA/Buchet-Chastel, 1982.

Fieschi, Jacques, ed. "Du Muet au parlant." Special issue. *Cinématographe* (May 1979), no. 47.

Gorbman, Claudia. *Unheard Melodies: Narrative Film Music*. Bloomington: Indiana University Press, 1987.

Henry, Jean-Jacques. "Notes sur le son chez Tati," *Cahiers du cinéma* (September 1979), no. 303.

"La Parole au cinéma/Speech in Film." *Iris* (1985), vol. 3, no. 1.

Larère, Odile. *De l'imaginaire au cinéma*. Paris: Albatros, 1980.

Leonardo da Vinci. *Notebooks of Leonardo Da Vinci*. Translation and introduction by Edward MacCurdy. New York: Reynal and Hitchcock, 1938.

Marie, Michel. "Son." In J. Collet, M. Marie, D. Percheron, J-P Simon, and M. Vernet, *Lectures du film*, pp. 198–210. Paris: Albatros, 1976.

—— "La Bouche bée," "Voix-off," special issue, ed. Marie-Claire Ropars-Wuilleumier, *Hors-cadre* (1985), no. 3.

Mott, R. L. *Sound Effects: Radio, TV, and Film*. Boston and London: Focal, 1990.

Merleau-Ponty, Maurice. *Phénoménologie de la perception*. Paris: Gallimard, 1976.

Odin, Roger. "A propos d'un couple de concepts: 'son in' vs. 'son off.' '' *Linguistique et sémiologie*, no. 6. Lyon: Presses Universitaires de Lyon, 1979.

Pinel, V. *Techniques du cinéma*. Coll. "Que sais-je?" no. 1873. Paris: Presses Universitaires de France, 1981.

Pommier, C. *Doublage et postsynchronisation: Cinéma et vidéo*. ed. Dujarric, 1988.

Reisz, Karel and Gavin Millar. *The Technique of Film Editing*. 2d ed. London and New York: Focal, 1968.

Ropars-Wuilleumier, Marie-Claire. *Le Texte divisé*. Paris: PUF, 1981.

Sacco, Christiane. *Plaidoyer au Roi de Prusse, ou la première anamorphose*. Paris: Buchet-Chastel, 1980.

Schaeffer, Pierre. *Traité des objets musicaux*. Rev. ed. Paris: Seuil, 1967.

Silverman, Kaja. *The Acoustic Mirror: The Female Voice in Psychoanalysis and Cinema*. Bloomington: Indiana University Press, 1988.

Straub, Jean-Marie and Danièle Huillet. "Entretien avec Jean-Marie Straub et Danièle Huillet." *Cahiers du cinéma* (August 1970), no. 223, pp. 48–57; *Cahiers du cinéma* (October 1970), no. 224, pp. 40–42.

Tati, Jacques (Serge Daney, J-J. Henry, S. Le Péron). "Entretiens avec Jacques Tati: 1. Le Son," *Cahiers du cinéma* (September 1979), no. 303, pp. 8–13.

Weis, Elisabeth. *The Silent Scream: Alfred Hitchcock's Sound Track*. Rutherford, N.J.: Fairleigh Dickinson University Press, 1982.

Weis, Elisabeth and John Belton, eds. *Film Sound: Theory and Practice*. New York: Columbia University Press, 1985.

Wurtzler, Steve. " 'She Sang Live But the Microphone Was Turned Off': The Live, the Recorded, and the Subject of Representation." In Rick Altman, ed., *Sound Theory/Sound Practice*, pp. 87–103. New York: Routledge, 1992.

INDEX

punctuative, 49; in *The Sacrifice*, 123–24; string tremolo in, 20; tempo in, 15; *see also* Opera

Musical films, 151, 184

Musical performances, 79, 91

Music videos, 37, 82, 151–52, 163, 165–68

Musique concrète, xvi, 137, 143

Muybridge, Eadweard, 61

Napoleon (film), 41, 67

Naturalism, 93, 94, 95, 119–20; *see also* Fidelity; Verisimilitude

Nielsen, Asta, x–xi

Nights of Cabiria (film), 133

Noise: anempathetic effect from, 9; auditory units of, 45; in early sound films, 148; materializing indices and, 115; multitrack recording and, 144–47, 155; in *Persona*, 205; silence expressed through, 57; vocal, 120–21

Nondiegetic sound, 73

Nouvelle vague (film), 46, 153

Offscreen sound, *see* Acousmatic sound

"Offscreen trash," 84–85

Oliveira, Manoel de, 16

Once Upon a Time in the West (film), 82

The One-Eyed Man (film), 129

One from the Heart (film), 153

Onscreen sound, 73

On-the-air sound, 76–77, 92

Opera: anempathetic music in, 8; *The Informer* as, 52, 53; integration, 184; Leone and, 82; pit music and, 80; silent films and, 48; string tremolo in, 20; synchronization in, 54

Ophuls, Max, 177, 182; *Earrings of Madame de*, 46; *Lola Montès*, 67; *Le Plaisir*, 66, 116, 181; *Tendre ennemie*, 129

Othon (film), 68, 69, 106

Pagnol, Marcel, 102

Paradjanov, Sergei, 158

The Passenger (film), 9, 77

Passive offscreen sound, 85–86

Peckinpah, Sam, 17, 62

Peignot, Jérôme, 71

Pelléas et Mélisande (Debussy), 51

Perception, 33–34, 44, 108; auditory, 9–11, 12–13, 90, 136, 182; of depth, xx–xxi, 71; of movement, 9–10, 11–12, 122, 134–35, 194; of speed, 9–10, 134–35; of time, 13–20; visual, 9–11, 12, 122, 136, 149, 182

Persona (film), *see* Bergman, Ingmar

Persona: The Transcendent Image (Blackwell), 220n2

Pettersson, P. O., 198

Phantom audio-vision, xix, 123–37, 218

Philosophical dualism, 218n2a

Phonogeny, 101–4

Photogeny, 102–3

Pitch (music), 30, 121

Pit music, 80, 81, 146

Le Plaisir (film), 66, 116, 181

Playtime (film), 180

Point of audition, 89–92, 93, 195